Annotated Teacher's Edition

WRITE SOURCE

Inside Writing Skills
Instruction and Practice

. . . a resource of student activities
to accompany

Inside Writing
Level 6

WRITE SOURCE®

GREAT SOURCE EDUCATION GROUP
a Houghton Mifflin Company
Wilmington, Massachusetts

A Few Words About
Inside Writing Skills: Level 6

Before you begin . . .

Inside Writing Skills provides you with opportunities to practice the editing and proofreading skills presented in the *Inside Writing* units.

Activities

Each skills activity includes a brief introduction to the topic and examples showing how to complete the activity. The first section, "Proofreading Activities," focuses on punctuation, on the mechanics of writing, and on usage. The second section, "Sentence Activities," provides practice in sentence combining and in correcting common sentence problems. The third section addresses the parts of speech. Many exercises include a **Next Step** activity that provides follow-up work, often in the form of a brief writing assignment.

Proofreader's Guide

The "Proofreader's Guide" (pages 149-186) presents the basic rules for punctuation, capitalization, spelling, and grammar. Activities are cross-referenced to the information in this part of the book to help you complete your work. You can also turn to this guide whenever you have an editing or proofreading question when you write.

Authors: Pat Sebranek and Dave Kemper

Trademarks and trade names are shown in this book strictly for illustrative purposes and are the property of their respective owners. The authors' references herein should not be regarded as affecting their validity.

Great Source and **Write Source** are registered trademarks of Houghton Mifflin Company.

Printed in the United States of America

International Standard Book Number: 0-669-50021-6 (student edition)

1 2 3 4 5 6 7 8 9 10 -POO- 10 09 08 07 06 05 04 03 02

International Standard Book Number: 0-669-50022-4 (teacher's edition)

1 2 3 4 5 6 7 8 9 10 -POO- 10 09 08 07 06 05 04 03 02

Inside Writing SKILLS

Proofreading Activities

Marking Punctuation

Editing for Mechanics

Commonly Misused Words

Sentence Activities

Understanding Sentences

Sentence Problems

Sentence Combining

Parts of Speech Activities

Nouns

Pronouns

Verbs

Adjectives and Adverbs

Interjections and Prepositions

Conjunctions

Proofreader's Guide

You will turn to this section to find information to help with each of the skills activities. You will find page numbers for the "Proofreader's Guide" in the upper right-hand corner of each exercise. You may also use this handy reference to find answers when you have questions about punctuation and grammar in your own writing.

Proofreading Activities

The activities in this section include sentences that need to be checked for punctuation, mechanics, and correct word choice. For more information and examples, all of the activities include page references to the "Proofreader's Guide." In addition, the **Next Step** activities encourage follow-up practice of certain skills.

End Punctuation 1

Periods, question marks, and exclamation points are used at the ends of sentences. Usually, these marks will mean that you have come to the end of a complete thought—either a statement or a question. (See pages 150 and 151 in the "Proofreader's Guide.")

■ **Period**

A period marks the end of a complete thought.

Many families have pets.

■ **Question Mark**

A question mark indicates a question.

What is your favorite animal?

■ **Exclamation Point**

An exclamation point expresses strong feelings or emphasis.

"Thanks for getting me a puppy!" Daniel shouted.

Note: In dialogue, you may need to use more than one end punctuation mark.

Directions ▶ Add the correct end punctuation marks to the following sentences. The first sentence has been done for you.

1. Cats are the most popular pet in this country_._

2. Why are cats our favorite pets_?_

3. Cats can take care of themselves with just a little help from people_._

4. Some cats are skilled mice-catchers_._

5. If my little brother ever sees a mouse, he yells, "Eeek_!_"

6. My parents wanted to give my little brother a surprise_._

7. Then my brother cheered, "Wow, a cat_!_"

8. I asked him, "Was it a surprise_?_"

9. "Was it ever_!_" he exclaimed_._

Next Step: Write three sentences about pets or other animals—one that ends with a period, one that ends with a question mark, and one that ends with an exclamation point.

End Punctuation 2

Proofreader's Guide
150, 151

Sentences end with periods, question marks, and exclamation points. Usually it's not hard to decide which one to use. Sometimes, though, the sentences require a little more thought. (For more information, see the "Proofreader's Guide.")

■ **Period**

A period marks the end of a complete thought.

We were planning our class trip.

■ **Question Mark**

A question mark ends a question in dialogue, or written conversation.

Bill asked, "Who has a suggestion?"

■ **Exclamation Point**

An exclamation point shows strong feelings in dialogue.

La Von called out, "I'd love to go to the aquarium!"

Directions ▶ Add the correct end punctuation marks to the following sentences. The first sentence has been done for you.

1   It was time to plan our class trip_._   Wow, what a hard decision _!_

2   Stuart asked Lisabeth, "Where did your brother's class go_?_"

3   "They went to the aquarium," she said_._

4   "What a great idea_!_" said Tasha_._   Other students suggested the

5   science museum or the zoo_._   Lisabeth said she likes to see colorful tropical

6   fish_._   Tasha said she wanted to check out the sea otters at the zoo_._

7   Lisabeth asked LaVon, "Where do you think we should go_?_" In the

8   end, we had three choices_._

9   Stuart asked the class, "How many people would like to go to the

10 aquarium_?_" The majority of us voted for the aquarium_._

Next Step: Write about a class trip you took. Use some questions and exclamations.

Commas with Dates, Numbers, Addresses, Direct Address

Proofreader's Guide
151, 152

Commas make writing easier to read because they keep words, numbers, and ideas from running together. Understanding how to use commas is one of the best writing skills you can master. (Turn to the "Proofreader's Guide" for more on commas.)

■ To Keep Numbers Clear

Commas are used in numbers of four or more digits to keep the numbers clear.

1,500 apples   **36,000,000 stars**

■ In Dates and Addresses

I will be 12 years old on **January 2, 2010**.
(Do not use a comma if only the month and year are written—"January 2010.")
I live at 634 Elm Street, Hamilton, Ohio 45011.
(Do not use a comma to separate the state from the ZIP code.)

■ In Direct Address

A noun of direct address names the person being spoken to.
Please answer the phone, Marlene.
(A comma separates a noun of direct address from the rest of the sentence.)

> **Directions** ▶ Using the rules described above as your guide, add commas as needed to the following sentences.

1. The store is located at 144 Landis Road, Raleigh, North Carolina 27609.

2. Students sold 1,399 tickets to the school play.

3. Raymond, you should learn to play the guitar.

4. The game will be played at 330 Park Road, Springville, Alabama.

5. On July 4, 2006, the United States will be 230 years old.

6. Frank, would you help Costas repair his scooter?

7. The ship will leave the harbor on August 25, 2003.

1. Tom Smith was asked to write a 1,500-word article for the school newsletter.

2. Other sixth graders volunteered to work on the special newsletter for September 20, 2002.

3. Ms. Lewis asked, "Will you get some paper, Sari?"

4. Ms. Lewis has been in charge of the newsletter since April 10, 2002.

5. Students raised $1,500 at bake sales during the previous school year to help pay for the newsletter.

6. By October 10, 2002, they hope to raise another $2,100 to meet expenses.

7. Gabrielle noted that the equipment they need would cost $2,975.

8. Tom said, "Gabrielle, thanks for the information."

9. "Tom, you'll have to write about 1,600 words every month," Gabrielle informed him.

10. Ms. Lewis said, "When we're finished, we'll send everything to the printing office at 621 Tyler Road, Scranton, Pennsylvania."

11. "Students, can we have the next issue ready by October 25, 2002?" asked Ms. Lewis.

12. One student wants to send a copy to his friend at 295 Spring Street, Sparta, Wisconsin 54656.

Next Step: Write two sentences with numbers needing commas and two sentences with nouns of direct address. Compare sentences in class.

Commas with Phrases, Clauses, Interruptions

Of all the punctuation marks, the one that has the most uses (and probably causes the most confusion) is the comma. Here are two more ways to use commas:

■ **To Separate Introductory Phrases and Clauses**

A comma is used to separate a long phrase or a clause that comes *before* the main part of the sentence.

At seven o'clock that night, we found the lost bike.
(This sentence begins with an introductory phrase.)

While we were downtown, we checked out the new music store.
(This sentence begins with an introductory clause.)

■ **To Set Off Interruptions**

Commas are used to set off words or phrases that interrupt a sentence.

In fact, we had a great time listening to the latest CD's.
(One comma follows an interruption at the beginning of a sentence.)

We had a great time, in fact, listening to the latest CD's.
(Commas come before and after an interruption in the middle of a sentence.)

> **Directions** ▶ Add commas as needed in each sentence below. The first sentence has been done for you.

1. When I am not doing homework, I like to listen to music.

2. Although my parents don't mind my music, they say it's too loud.

3. Actually, I play my CD's at low volume.

4. Of all the musical styles, I like alternative rock the best.

5. Because my sister prefers classical music, we don't listen together.

6. My sister's CD's are cheaper, to be sure.

7. After every trip to the music store, she has extra money.

8. For the same money, in fact, she can buy twice as many CD's.

9. Along with the CD's, she buys sheet music.

Add commas as needed in the following sentences. The first sentence has been done for you.

1. When the United States became an independent country, its leaders decided to build a capital city.

2. Because a capital is the seat of government, its location is very important.

3. Although several U.S. cities had served as the capital, government officials decided to look for another location.

4. While many people had opinions about where the capital should be, the leaders in Congress wanted to build a new city.

5. In fact, the leaders received some land from Virginia and Maryland.

6. Moreover, they hired Pierre L'Enfant to draw up a city plan with many broad streets.

7. Although the District of Columbia is the capital of the United States, many people say it looks like a European city.

8. After some deliberation, L'Enfant decided to divide the city into four sections.

9. In just a short time, a visitor can visit monuments dedicated to many famous people.

10. For those unafraid of heights, the Washington Monument provides a dramatic view of the White House and the Capitol Building.

11. Washington, D.C., is unique because it is, after all, the only city in the nation that is not part of a state.

Next Step: Write two sentences about the street where you live. Use introductory phrases or interruptions in each sentence. Exchange your work with a partner. Make sure your partner has used commas correctly.

Commas to Set Off Appositives

An **appositive** is a word or phrase that renames a noun that comes before the appositive. Place commas before and after appositives that come in the middle of a sentence. Place a comma before an appositive at the end of a sentence.

Logan Park Zoo, the biggest zoo in my state, has amazing trained seals.

("The biggest zoo in my state" is an appositive because it renames the proper noun "Logan Park Zoo.")

My favorite seal is Sparky, a veteran performer.

("A veteran performer" renames the noun "Sparky.")

Directions ➤ Use commas to set off appositives in the sentences below. The first sentence has been done for you.

1. My favorite place, the Logan Park Zoo, is not far from my house.

2. Jenna, one of my little sisters, likes to go there with me.

3. I have made friends with Mrs. Bailey, one of the zoo workers.

4. My favorite animals, the seals and the otters, all swim in one big pool.

5. We go to the arena, the best place to see the animals in action.

6. If we see Maya, the seal trainer, she will get us a good seat.

7. Ringo, the biggest seal, often grabs the most fish.

8. Then we run to see Jenna's favorite animals, the lions.

9. They live in the African Plain, a special section in the zoo.

10. I told Ms. Rodriguez, my science teacher, that I will report on the seals.

11. Now I can write about my firsthand experiences with seals for science, my favorite class.

Next Step: Create three sentences that include appositive phrases. The first sentence should tell something about a family member; the second should tell about a friend; and the third should tell about a place you like to go. Exchange sentences with a classmate.

Commas in a Series and Within Compound Sentences

Here are two common uses of commas.

■ Between Items in a Series

Use commas to separate words or phrases in a series. A series contains at least three words or phrases in a row.

The concert was loud, exciting, and crowded.

("Loud," "exciting," and "crowded" are three words in a series.)

■ In Compound Sentences

Use a comma before the connecting word in a compound sentence. A compound sentence is made up of two or more independent clauses—simple sentences—connected by words like *and, but, so, or,* and *yet.*

I like drums, and they are especially important to marching bands.

("I like drums" and "they are especially important to marching bands" are independent clauses.)

> **Directions** ▶ **Use commas as needed in the sentences below. The first sentence has been done for you.**

1. I must decide whether to study the trumpet, the violin, or the clarinet.

2. Music is my favorite subject, and I want to play in the school band.

3. Orchestra instruments include strings, woodwinds, brass, and percussion.

4. Violins, violas, cellos, and double basses make up the string section.

5. I like the sound of the cello, but I don't want to carry it around.

6. My friend plays the cello, and she said, "It's hard to take it on the bus."

7. I could play a brass instrument like the trumpet, cornet, or trombone.

8. I like the saxophone, yet I enjoy the trombone.

9. I may choose the trumpet, but I'm just not ready to decide.

Next Step: Write a question that contains at least three items in a series. Then write an answer to the question using a compound sentence. Use commas correctly.

Comma Review 1

Proofreader's Guide
151-154

Use commas to separate a longer phrase or clause that comes before the main part of the sentence and to set off an appositive phrase from the rest of the sentence. (An appositive phrase renames the noun or pronoun before it.)

Directions ▶ In the following sentences, use commas where needed. The first sentence has been done for you.

1. The raccoon, a medium-sized mammal, is a familiar forest animal.

2. In most parts of North America, you will find raccoons.

3. Above a light-gray undercoat, the raccoon's longer and stiffer hairs are dark gray.

4. A raccoon, a patient hunter, can catch almost anything for dinner.

5. At the ends of their long fingers, raccoons have sharp claws.

6. Raccoons sit at the edge of the water or wade into shallow streams to catch fish, one of their favorite foods.

7. Because raccoons can eat many different things, they can successfully raise many young.

8. After their birth in early summer, baby raccoons soon start exploring.

9. During their first year, raccoon babies stay with their mother in the den, their home for the winter.

10. Raccoons are nocturnal animals, creatures resting most of the day and searching for food at night.

Next Step: Write two sentences about an animal. Use an appositive in one sentence and a long introductory phrase or clause in the other one.

Comma Review 2

Use commas between items in a series, between independent clauses, and between items in dates and addresses.

> **Directions** ⟩ In the following sentences, add commas where needed. The first one has been done for you.

1. John Fitzgerald Kennedy was born on May 29,1917, in Boston, Massachusetts.

2. The Kennedy family was very important in Boston politics,and John Kennedy followed the family tradition.

3. John Kennedy's father was a businessman,an ambassador,and an investor in the motion picture industry.

4. The Kennedy sons included Joseph,John,Robert,and Edward.

5. John Kennedy completed his education at Harvard,and then he ran for public office in Boston.

6. John Kennedy won the 1960 presidential election,and he became the first Roman Catholic president of the United States.

7. The popular vote was very close,but Kennedy beat Richard Nixon.

8. On January 20,1961,Kennedy was inaugurated.

9. Kennedy's cabinet included Secretary of State Dean Rusk,Secretary of Labor Arthur Goldberg,and Attorney General Robert Kennedy.

10. The first lady,Jacqueline Kennedy,became known for her sense of style,ability to speak French and Spanish,and desire for privacy.

11. On November 22,1963,President Kennedy was killed in Dallas,Texas.

Semicolons and Colons 1

A semicolon (**;**) can be used to join two independent clauses when no connecting word is used. It can also be used when two independent clauses are joined by a conjunctive adverb (*however, instead, therefore, as a result, in addition,* and so on). A colon (**:**) may be used to introduce a list.

■ **Semicolon to Join Two Independent Clauses**

My family moved to a new house; I loved it.
(Each clause can stand alone as a separate sentence.)

■ **Semicolon to Join Two Independent Clauses Connected by a Conjunctive Adverb**

I liked the old house; however, it was small.
(The semicolon comes before the conjunctive adverb "however.")

■ **Colon to Introduce a List of Words and Phrases**

The East Coast has many big cities: New York, Philadelphia, and Baltimore.
("The East Coast has many big cities" introduces a list of cities.)

> **Directions** Add semicolons or colons as needed in the following sentences. The first one has been done for you.

1. Five students wished to be treasurer**:** Lucy, Claude, Ray, Amad, and Shavon.

2. Others were interested**;** however, no one else decided to run for office.

3. Claude got the most votes**;** therefore, he was declared the winner.

4. Claude had promised three things**:** more school dances, a big picnic in June, and money left over at the end of the year.

5. He is doing a good job so far**;** let's see how he continues.

6. Amad agreed to help Claude**;** the two have worked well together.

1. The school board will decide among three locations for the new school building: Grove Avenue, City Center Plaza, or Perkins Drive.

2. People thought that the school would be on Grove Avenue; however, traffic would be a problem at that location.

3. Some people wanted to build the school there anyway; instead, the parents' association suggested two other places.

4. These people made suggestions: Mr. Clemons, Ms. Wilmot, and Dr. Fitch.

5. Then Reverend Kramer said, "The location on Perkins Drive has very little traffic and is near a park; therefore, it may be ideal."

Next Step: Follow the directions below to write your own sentences. Share them with the class. *Answers will vary.*

1. Use a colon in a sentence that introduces a list of three or four things. Use the phrase "the following items" or "the following people."

   The following people volunteered to work today: George, Greg, Lindsay,

   and Maya.

2. Use a semicolon in a sentence that joins two independent clauses with the word "however" or "therefore."

   He planned to hike early Tuesday; however, the rain made hiking

   dangerous.

3. Use a semicolon in a short sentence that contains two independent clauses without a connecting word.

   She loves doing her best; she always hands in excellent work.

Semicolons and Colons 2

When you write, it is important to use semicolons and colons correctly. The following rule is a good one to know:

■ **To Separate Groups of Words Containing Commas**

The items in Jackie's purse include lip balm, moisturizer, and hand cleaner; pens, pencils, and paper; and a phone card, a library card, and an identification card.

Directions ▶ Add semicolons and colons as needed in the following sentences. If a sentence is correct, write "C" on the line.

____ **1.** Alaska can be cold in summer ⋀ Florida can be hot in winter.

____ **2.** Temperatures below 32 degrees can occur in Idaho in August ⋀ however, in the Florida Keys such temperatures never occur.

____ **3.** Freezing weather rarely occurs in parts of several states ⋀ Texas, Florida, Louisiana, and Arizona.

____ **4.** California has different climate zones ⋀ the inland valleys, the southern coast, and the northern mountains.

_C_ **5.** Frost comes early in the northern plains states, but it comes much later in the southeast.

____ **6.** The earliest freezing temperatures occur in these western states ⋀ Oregon, Idaho, Montana, Wyoming, and Colorado.

____ **7.** I have lived in these places ⋀ Iona, Idaho ⋀ Milo, Maine ⋀ and Ida, Iowa.

____ **8.** On cold winter days in those cities, we enjoyed vegetable, chicken, or bean soup ⋀ chicken, beef, or pork pies ⋀ and warm homemade bread.

____ **1.** People often think hares and rabbits are the same animal₍;₎ however, hares are different from rabbits.

____ **2.** Hares have large ears with black tips₍;₎ rabbits have shorter ears.

____ **3.** Both hares and rabbits have similar features₍:₎ large ears, short tails, and long back legs for hopping.

____ **4.** Hares are born with their eyes open₍;₎ rabbits are born with their eyes closed.

_C_ **5.** Rabbits and hares can live in different kinds of climates: cold, moderate, rainy, and dry.

____ **6.** They can also adapt to most conditions₍;₎ the one type of weather that they cannot tolerate is extreme heat with humidity.

____ **7.** I saw these three animals at the zoo₍:₎ Trooper, a rabbit₍;₎ Jack, a jackrabbit₍;₎ and Leaper, a snowshoe hare.

Next Step: Follow the directions below to write your own sentences.

1. Write a sentence in which you use a colon to introduce a list of things.

These are my favorite colors: red, blue, and green.

_____

2. Write a sentence that contains a list of things but doesn't need a colon.

I like to run, hike, and swim.

_____

Punctuating Dialogue 1

In the following sentences, quotation marks set off the speaker's words. As you will see, a comma separates the speaker's words from the rest of the sentence.

> **The man asked, "Where is Main Street?"**
> **"Go straight ahead, and then turn left at the light," said Louis. "You'll see it."**
> **"Thanks. I appreciate it," the man added.**

(In written conversation, quotation marks are used to set off a speaker's exact words. A comma is often used to separate the speaker's words from the rest of the sentence.)

Directions ▶ Put quotation marks in the following sentences. The first sentence has been done for you.

1   Lana asked, "When can we sign up for the class trip, Mr. Ray?"

2   "Did you ask your parents yet, Lana?" he responded. "I have to be

3   sure that it's OK with them," he continued.

4   "Yes, I did, Mr. Ray," Lana said. "They definitely want me to go on

5   the trip."

6   Mr. Ray said, "I will be collecting the permission slips next week."

7   "Can I give you mine now?" Lana said. "I might forget later."

8   "I hope you won't forget to come early on the day of the trip," Mr.

9   Ray laughed. "The bus will be leaving at 7:00 a.m."

10 "Maybe I should write a note to myself, Mr. Ray," Lana answered.

11 "I think you better do that," he said.

Next Step: Think of a conversation you have had recently—about a TV program, current events, a sporting event, or something else. Write down what you remember of the conversation, using quotation marks correctly.

Punctuating Dialogue 2

You know it's easy to talk with friends and family members. After all, you've had a lot of practice. However, you may not be as skilled when it comes to recording a conversation on paper. Knowing the following punctuation rules can help:

"Ted, please deliver this note to the office," said Ms. Tower.
(In written conversation, quotation marks are used to set off a speaker's exact words. A comma is often used to separate the speaker's words from the rest of the sentence.)

"Should I do it right now?" José asked.
(Here a question mark indicates that the speaker's exact words ask a question.)

"I would like that," Ms. Tower said. **"Thanks."**
(A period comes after "said" because that's the end of a complete sentence.)

"Okay," said José, **"I'll finish my assignment later."**
(A comma comes after "José" because what follows completes the sentence.)

> **Directions** ⟩ Read the following sentences carefully. Then write your own sentences, using each sample as a model. Make sure to punctuate each sentence correctly. *Answers will vary.*

1. "The dentist will see you in a few moments," the receptionist told Lee.

   "You can have a seat in the meantime," she said.
   _____

   _____

2. Lee's sister asked her, "Do you want me to wait here with you?"

   Shannon questioned, "Do you have your phone with you?"
   _____

   _____

3. "No, you may go," Lee told her sister. "I'm fine."

   "Okay, I'll see you later," she replied. "I'll watch for you."
   _____

   _____

Next Step: Exchange papers with a partner and check one another's sentences. Then try writing a short dialogue with a partner. Choose a topic and record your conversation.

Punctuating Dialogue 3

Remember that quotation marks set off the exact words of the speaker. A comma separates the speaker's words from the rest of the sentence. Finally, end punctuation marks usually go inside the quotation marks.

Directions ⟩⟩ Use end punctuation marks, commas, and quotation marks to punctuate the following sentences. The first sentence has been done for you.

1. "Would you like to help me make something special?" Ivy's mother asked.

2. "You said you would like to cook more, so let's do it together," she added.

3. Ivy asked, "How much time will it take, Mom?"

4. "You have plenty of time," her mother said, "before you have to leave."

5. "What will we need, Mom, to make this dish?" Ivy asked.

6. "Get the bread, some butter, and an egg," her mother replied.

7. Ivy's mother told her, "This is like a fried egg, but we cut a hole in the bread and put the egg in the hole."

8. "Do we fry the bread with the egg until the egg is done?" asked Ivy.

9. "Yes," said her mother. "I will be sure the egg doesn't break."

10. Ivy asked, "What kind of pan will we use?"

11. "We will use this special square pan," her mother said.

12. Ivy exclaimed, "This is the square egg you always talked about Mom!"

13. "That's right, Ivy," her mother said. "I know you will like it."

Next Step: Write down a conversation about food or cooking—a real one between you and your partner or one you make up. Be sure to punctuate each sentence correctly.

Punctuating Titles 1

Proofreader's Guide
157, 159

Use italics or underlining to indicate the titles of books, plays, magazines, movies, TV shows, record albums, CD's, newspapers, and for the names of ships and aircraft. Use quotation marks for titles of songs, poems, short stories, articles, episodes of TV programs, and for book chapters.

Where the Sidewalk Ends is my favorite poetry book. (book title)

"On Wisconsin" is a popular school song. (song title)

> **Directions** Correctly punctuate the titles in the following sentences. The first sentence has been done for you.

1. My parents like to watch old episodes of <u>I Love Lucy</u> on TV.

2. We sometimes sing "The Star-Spangled Banner" at school.

3. At the airport, I have seen many people reading <u>USA Today</u>.

4. You can read about celebrities in <u>People</u> magazine.

5. In our science class, Ms. Lukas shows us <u>Scientific American</u> magazine.

6. My sister's favorite book is <u>Superfudge</u>.

7. The Beatles had a very famous album called <u>Abbey Road</u>.

8. My cousins used to watch <u>Sesame Street</u> on TV.

9. Have you read "The Gift of the Magi," a short story by O. Henry?

10. One chapter in <u>Bridge to Terabithia</u> is called "The Golden Room."

11. My grandmother gave me a subscription to <u>National Geographic</u> magazine.

12. A newspaper with a lot of information about the economy is the <u>Wall Street Journal</u>.

Next Step: Write three sentences that each include a title that is correctly underlined or in quotation marks. Have a classmate check your work.

Punctuating Titles 2

Proofreader's Guide
157, 159

The titles of longer pieces of writing (books, magazines, albums, movies, etc.) are italicized or underlined, while the titles of shorter pieces (short stories, articles, songs, poems, etc.) are placed in quotation marks.

Many young people have seen the movie <u>Lord of the Rings: Fellowship of the Ring</u>. (movie title)

"Mending Wall" is a poem by Robert Frost. (poem title)

Directions ▶ Correctly punctuate the titles in the following sentences. The first sentence has been done for you.

1. I have read parts of the book <u>The Collected Works of Edgar Allan Poe</u>.

2. I loved the short story "The Murders in the Rue Morgue."

3. Two other spooky short stories, "The Fall of the House of Usher" and "The Gold Bug," also were great!

4. Poe's poem "The Raven" is almost as spooky as the stories.

5. Other poems, like "To Helen" and "Anabelle Lee," are more romantic.

6. My mom saw an old horror movie on TV that was based on Poe's story "The Tell-Tale Heart."

7. She saw the movie on the weekly program <u>The Saturday Night Movie</u>.

8. A movie review titled "The Week of the Horror Film" published in the <u>Philadelphia Daily Herald</u> said the movie was a Poe "classic."

9. I also found out that Poe wrote "Eldorado," a song about the gold rush.

10. To earn a living, Poe was an editor at <u>Graham's Magazine</u>.

11. If I wrote a play about Poe's work, I'd call it <u>Songs and Nightmares</u>.

Punctuating Dialogue and Titles Review

Directions ⟩ Punctuate the dialogue and the titles in the following sentences. The first sentence has been done for you.

1 "Carmen," the teacher asked, "what stories did you like to read when

2 you were younger?"

3   "Mr. Penney, that was so long ago. I'm not sure I can remember,"

4 Carmen answered.

5   Mr. Penney said, "Think back. I'm sure you can remember one

6 story."

7   Carmen recalled that she had liked "Cinderella" and "Snow White."

8 "I liked the movie versions of the stories about Cinderella and Snow

9 White and their princes," Carmen said. "They had great music, too."

10 "Can you think of any songs?" he asked.

11   Carmen remembered the song "Bippety Boppity Boo." She said,

12 "I remember some songs. But I can't sing them, Mr. Penney." Carmen

13 also mentioned that she liked the poem "Little Boy Blue."

14   Mr. Penney smiled and said, "You have a great memory, Carmen."

15 For some reason, his comment made her think about the song "Under

16 the Sea" from the movie The Little Mermaid.

Next Step: Think of a conversation you have had with a friend. Write it as a dialogue, using quotation marks correctly.

Hyphens 1

Use a hyphen (-) to make some compound words and to divide a word at the end of a line. You should divide a word only between syllables.

■ **To Form Compound Words**

A seven-month-old kitten

CD-ROM

Tari's sixth-grade teacher

Luke's brother-in-law

■ **To Divide Words at the End of a Line**

run-ning   key-hole   along-side   im-me-di-ate

> **Directions** > Use hyphens as needed in the following sentences. The first sentence has been done for you.

1. We have a three-week plan to make our team better.

2. Some people love worn-out jeans.

3. The three-week-old container of milk in the refrigerator smells bad.

4. Her six-year-old sister is with the baby-sitter.

5. Jobie's sister-in-law is a chef.

6. Jill's husband-to-be bought her a beautiful necklace.

> **Directions** > Using hyphens, divide the following words into syllables. (Check your answers in a dictionary.) The first one has been done for you.

1. processor   _pro-ces-sor_   6. rainbow   _rain-bow_

2. collapse   _col-lapse_   7. jackal   _jack-al_

3. fantastic   _fan-tas-tic_   8. underline   _un-der-line_

4. impossible   _im-pos-si-ble_   9. umbrella   _um-brel-la_

5. satisfy   _sat-is-fy_   10. quarrel   _quar-rel_

Hyphens 2

Use hyphens between the numbers of a fraction written as a word, and with some prefixes (*all, ex, self, great*) and suffixes (*elect* and *free*).

■ **To Write Fractions as Words**

   Fred ran four-fifths of a mile yesterday.

■ **To Form New Words**

   He is the ex-champion miler of our school.

   Josie is the president-elect of our student council.

Directions ➤ Use hyphens where needed in the following sentences. The first sentence has been done for you.

1. The bank is paying one-half percent interest on checking accounts.

2. Tullia Marolo is Martha's great-grandmother.

3. The ex-prime minister of England is still active in politics.

4. Some people are very self-centered.

5. My father looks for foods that are totally fat-free.

6. Three-quarters of the students in my class are taking Spanish.

7. Listening to music is my all-time favorite thing to do on weekends.

Next Step: Write a sentence that answers each of the following questions. In each response, use a hyphen and the prefix or suffix indicated in parentheses.

1. Who is Bill Clinton? *(ex)*

   Bill Clinton is an ex-president of the United States.

2. What does the word "silent" mean? *(free)*

   The word means noise-free.

3. How is the mother of your grandmother related to you? *(great)*

   She is my great-grandmother.

Apostrophes 1

Use apostrophes to make contractions and to show possession or ownership.

■ **To Form Contractions**

The apostrophe used in a contraction shows that one or more letters have been left out.

can't (can + not)   **we're** (we + are)

■ **To Form Singular Possessives**

Form the possessive of most singular nouns by adding an apostrophe and *s*.

Tarsha's book   **Sylvia's glasses**

■ **To Form Plural Possessives**

Form the possessive of plural nouns ending in *s* by adding just an apostrophe. For plural nouns not ending in *s*, add an apostrophe and *s*.

the cats' bowls   **the women's purses**

■ **To Show Shared Possession**

When possession is shared, add an apostrophe and *s* to the last noun.

France and Germany's border

> **Directions** ▶ Add apostrophes as needed in the following sentences. Refer to the examples above as a guide. The first one has been done for you.

1. Claire and Julia's house was painted yellow last week.

2. It doesn't feel like summer yet; it isn't warm enough.

3. Scrooge's food supply is getting low.

4. The three friends' pictures arrived at the store.

5. We shouldn't forget to take care of Gina's plants before we leave.

6. The men's shoe department moved from the first to the third floor.

7. It was Mondo's idea to clean his room.

8. You'll find your keys in the morning.

9. Marla and Niko's science teacher has a pet tarantula.

         kids'

1   All the neighborhood ~~kid's~~ Halloween costumes were terrific this year!

2   Chrissy Towne's idea was to dress like a ball of thread, carrying a pin

3   cushion and needles. Her brother Todd was one of several boys who wore a

       Knight's   *hadn't*

4   Jedi ~~Knights'~~ outfit. Terell ~~had'nt~~ seen the latest *Star Wars* movie, but he

5   tried to look like C3PO. Elon Langley from the next street had on her older

                         didn't

6   sister's basketball uniform. Her friend Kali ~~did'nt~~ mind lending her a pair

7   of basketball shoes. Teel Jenkin was dressed like a dalmatian dog with

                   Grace's

8   black spots, and her cousin ~~Graces'~~ zebra outfit was also black and white.

9   Mr. Tompkins told us that we all lived up to our neighborhood's reputation

                                              hadn't

10   for unusual costumes! We were happy to hear that we ~~hadnt'~~ failed in our

11   efforts.

Next Step: Write three or four sentences that describe a costume or uniform you once wore. Be sure that each sentence contains at least one word with an apostrophe. Exchange papers with a partner and check for apostrophe errors.

Apostrophes 2

The possessive of most singular nouns is formed by adding an apostrophe and an *s*.

The cat likes to eat out of the dog's dish.
(The dish belongs to the dog.)

Rosario's outfit was brand-new.
(The outfit belongs to Rosario.)

Proofreader's Guide
158, 159

Directions ▶ Use the singular possessive form of each of the following words in a sentence. The first one has been done for you.

1. computer

My computer's mouse isn't working.

2. shoes

My shoe's heel is practically worn flat.

3. *(any kind of food)*

The buffalo taco's flavor was unusual.

4. *(name of a place)*

Disneyland's streets are always swept and clean.

5. *(name of a person)*

Meesha's book is wrapped in blue paper.

6. *(topic of your choice)*

Answers will vary.

Punctuation Review 1

This exercise reviews various types of punctuation such as commas, semicolons, colons, apostrophes, quotation marks, and underlining.

> **Directions** ▶ Correct the punctuation in the following sentences. (The information in parentheses tells you what kind of errors to look for.) The first one has been done for you.

1. The writer Katherine Paterson, author of <u>Bridge to Terabithia</u>, was born in China. *(punctuating titles)*

2. Paterson's parents were born in America, and they returned when Katherine was in elementary school. *(using apostrophes and commas)*

3. She learned Chinese while in China; however, she did not use it again for many years. *(using semicolons and commas)*

4. While living in Japan, she studied Japanese. *(using commas)*

5. Paterson has lived in the states of Tennessee, Virginia, and Vermont. *(using commas)*

6. She has raised four children: two boys and two girls. *(using colons)*

7. One of her novels, <u>Jacob Have I Loved</u>, is about two sisters named Caroline and Sarah Louise; much of it takes place on the Chesapeake Bay in Maryland. *(punctuating titles; using semicolons and commas)*

8. The sisters are twins; however, they never get along with each other. *(using semicolons and commas)*

9. Paterson has said, "I don't always write about characters who do or say things that I approve of." *(punctuating dialogue)*

Punctuation Review 2

This exercise reviews several types of punctuation: commas, semicolons, apostrophes, periods, quotation marks, hyphens, question marks, and exclamation points.

> **Directions** Proofread the following paragraphs. Add any needed punctuation. The first sentence has been done for you.

1   Our whole family, 20 of us in all, planned a summer trip to the

2   mountains for Granddad's 70th birthday. We met in Lake Tahoe,

3   California. Some of our cousins drove all the way from Texas; others

4   flew in from Iowa, Oregon, Tennessee, and Wisconsin. Everyone stayed in

5   a great big house in the hills. The house was over 7,000 feet above

6   sea level. With towering pine trees, rocks, and mountain peaks visible in

7   every direction, it was clear that we were way up in the Sierra Nevada

8   Mountains. In fact, we were so far up the hillside, we would have had

9   to hike downhill to get a ski lift. (or) !

10   "What shall we do today?" asked our grandfather. "How about a hike

11   around Emerald Bay?" After some debate, all the aunts, uncles, and

12   cousins got into Mark and Sandy's vans. We made our way down the

13   steep, winding roads. Then we carefully followed our route across the

14   valley to the southwest side of the lake. We were lucky; no one got

15   lost. Emerald Bay looked like the parking lot at a grocery store on the

16   day before Thanksgiving. It was full of parked cars and people waiting

17   to park; however, no one was leaving. Finally some spaces opened up

18 for us, and we were able to get out and have a look at the scenery.

19 We had a great view of the bay, the boats, and a little castle on

20 an island. Everything seemed to be floating on the deepest, clearest,

21 blue-green water you could imagine.

22   The sun was shining; the air was cool and refreshing. We were

23 rounded up and forced to pose for a family photograph. Dylan stood

24 behind his father-in-law, and he made faces at the camera. Some of us

25 wandered around the site; others admired the countryside. Everyone

26 found it hard to leave. The younger cousins took Chris's challenge and

27 followed a path over the rocks. Most of the older aunts and uncles

28 followed Granddad on a wide trail. After a while, everyone turned up at

29 the rocky shoreline and took some time to rest, enjoy the cold water,

30 and have a look around. Before too long, it was time to hike up to the

31 turnout where Bob and Sarah, our lazy cousins, were waiting in the

32 shade. "You missed the paddleboat," we cried.

33 "You didn't see the hawks in the trees," they replied. In the end, we

34 couldn't decide who had had the best time that day.

Next Step: Write a short descriptive paragraph about a trip you made with others or by yourself. Try to include some dialogue. Make sure you use commas, quotation marks, semicolons, hyphens, and apostrophes correctly.

Capitalization and Abbreviations

You know about capitalizing the first word in a sentence. You also know about capitalizing the specific names of places (*Phoenix, Korea, Illinois*) and persons (*Mr. Penney, Dr. Fuller, Carlos*).

It's also important to know how to use abbreviations, which are shortened forms of words and phrases. For instance, *Dr.* is the abbreviation for *Doctor.* A list of common abbreviations follows.

M.D. (Doctor of Medicine)

Ph.D. (Doctor of Philosophy)

U.S.A. (United States of America)

Mr. (Mister)   **Mrs. Ms.** (Mistress)

Directions ▶ In each of the following examples, correct any errors in capitalization and abbreviations by writing the correct form on the line. If the phrase is correct as stated, leave the line blank. The first one has been done for you.

1. president Monroe ___President___

2. ms Kwan ___Ms.___

3. New York yankees ___Yankees___

4. mayor Lawrence ___Mayor___

5. next July _____

6. north Dakota ___North___

7. the spanish coast ___Spanish___

8. ohio river___Ohio River___

9. the planet saturn ___Saturn___

10. spring 2002 _____

11. january 3 ___January___

12. mr. Mays ___Mr.___

13. Harris junior high ___Junior High___

14. dr martinez ___Dr. Martinez___

15. lake Michigan ___Lake___

16. 335 Prince street ___Street___

17. her Sister ___sister___

18. the Civil war ___War___

19. senator Grant ___Senator___

20. Trevor j Bennett ___J.___

Read each sentence below and put a line through any letter that should be either capitalized or lowercased. Then make a correction above each mistake. Also check abbreviations for correct punctuation. Hint: First make corrections you are sure about. Then go through the sentences again. The first one has been done for you.

1. You can see many ~~S~~ights if you walk along ~~f~~ifth ~~a~~venue in New York.

2. You will hear many languages, including ~~s~~panish, ~~f~~rench, ~~i~~talian, and ~~r~~ussian.

3. A famous toy store, F.ao Schwartz, is located at 767 ~~f~~ifth ~~a~~venue.

4. The ~~g~~uggenheim ~~m~~useum is located at ~~f~~ifth ~~a~~venue and 89th ~~s~~treet.

5. It was designed by the well-known architect Frank ~~l~~loyd ~~w~~right.

6. An institution called the ~~m~~etropolitan Museum of Art is at 82nd ~~s~~treet.

7. Ms. Colombo took us to the ~~M~~useum, which is really in ~~c~~entral ~~p~~ark.

8. Another interesting museum is the Cloisters in Fort Tryon ~~p~~ark.

9. The ~~p~~laza Hotel is on Fifth ~~a~~venue, right across the street from ~~c~~entral ~~p~~ark.

10. If you continue walking ~~D~~owntown, you'll see the ~~e~~mpire State Building.

11. Fifth ~~a~~venue ends at Washington Square Park.

12. People from all over Europe, ~~s~~outh America, and ~~a~~sia visit New York ~~c~~ity every day.

13. The Statue ~~O~~f ~~l~~iberty in New York ~~h~~arbor was designed by ~~b~~artholdi, a ~~f~~rench sculptor.

Next Step: Write a paragraph about a local library, museum, or other attraction. Do not capitalize any words. Then exchange papers with a classmate and correct any words that should be capitalized.

Capitalization 1

Proofreader's Guide
160-162

A proper noun names a specific person, place, thing, or idea. Proper nouns are always capitalized.

Coretta Scott King (specific person)

McKinley Middle School (specific place)

Chicago Tribune (specific thing—newspaper)

Bronze Age (specific period of time)

Father's Day (specific idea)

Directions　　Correct any errors in capitalization in the sentences below. The first sentence has been done for you.

1. A celebrated ~~A~~artist and ~~W~~writer for children today is ~~m~~Maurice ~~s~~Sendak.

2. His best-known book, *Where the ~~w~~Wild Things Are,* was published in 1963 when ~~s~~Sendak was 35 years old.

3. The hero in the book is named ~~m~~Max, who has to go to bed without his dinner.

4. Sendak was born in ~~b~~Brooklyn, ~~n~~New ~~y~~York, and always wanted to be an ~~A~~artist.

5. He liked to go into ~~m~~Manhattan to see all the tall buildings.

6. One of his early jobs was decorating windows in the famous toy store ~~f.a.o.~~FAO ~~s~~Schwartz.

7. He was just 19 years old when a book he co-authored, *~~a~~Atomics for the ~~m~~Millions,* was published.

8. Another book by ~~m~~Maurice ~~s~~Sendak is called *Really Rosie* because the author had a friend named ~~r~~Rose.

9. Sendak won a well-deserved award, the Caldecott, for ~~C~~children's ~~B~~book illustration.

Next Step: Write three sentences about a book you like. Include one or two proper nouns in each sentence, but do not capitalize them. Then exchange your sentences with a classmate and correct the capitalization in each other's work.

Capitalization 2

In addition to capitalizing the names of people and places, you should also capitalize the names of specific schools, school courses, languages, nationalities, periods of time, sections of the country, roads or highways, and nicknames of states.

Beginning Band (specific course)

Spanish (language and nationality)

Industrial Revolution (period of time)

Highway 41 (specific highway)

the Deep South (specific section of the country)

> **Directions**

Add capital letters as needed in the following sentences. (The number of capital letters needed is in parentheses at the end of each sentence.) The first one has been done for you.

1. Ohio is the ~~b~~Buckeye ~~s~~State, and ~~n~~New ~~j~~Jersey is the Garden ~~s~~State. *(5)*

2. My brother goes to the ~~u~~University of ~~m~~Maryland. *(2)*

3. He is taking history this year; last year he took ~~i~~Intermediate ~~s~~Spanish. *(2)*

4. He wants to study the ~~f~~French ~~r~~Revolution. *(2)*

5. Is ~~w~~Wrigley Field in the same city as Yankee ~~s~~Stadium? *(2)*

6. The planet nearest the sun is ~~m~~Mercury. *(1)*

7. Yiling speaks ~~c~~Chinese with her father, ~~d~~Dr. ~~c~~Chang. *(3)*

8. This year, ~~n~~New Year's ~~d~~Day is on a ~~m~~Monday. *(3)*

9. These fossils are from the ~~i~~Ice ~~a~~Age. *(2)*

10. People from the ~~m~~Midwest enjoy traveling to ~~f~~Florida during winter. *(2)*

11. Many people like to celebrate ~~j~~July 4th with fireworks. *(1)*

Next Step: Capitalize words such as *mother, father,* and *aunt* when they are used as names; do not capitalize these words if they come after *my, his, her, our,* etc. Write three sentences about members of your family using these rules. Exchange papers with a classmate and check each other's use of capitalization.

Abbreviations

An **abbreviation** is the shortened form of a word or phrase. Look at the examples below.

Mr. Carey (Mister)

Reed Ave. (Avenue)

Richmond, WV (West Virginia)

R.S.V.P. (French phrase meaning "please reply")

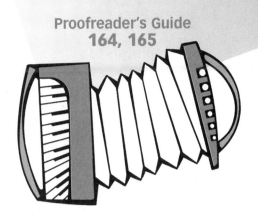

Directions ▶ Match the word in the first column with the correct abbreviation in the second column. The first one has been done for you.

<u>*d*</u> **1.** Parkway

<u>*f*</u> **2.** Boulevard

<u>*e*</u> **3.** Fort

<u>*c*</u> **4.** East

<u>*a*</u> **5.** Street

<u>*b*</u> **6.** Lane

a. St.

b. Ln.

c. E.

d. Pkwy.

e. Ft.

f. Blvd.

Directions ▶ Match the word or words in the first column with the correct abbreviation in the second column. Note that some common abbreviations do not have periods after them.

<u>*g*</u> **1.** quart

<u>*a*</u> **2.** kilometer

<u>*e*</u> **3.** pound

<u>*f*</u> **4.** Doctor of Medicine

<u>*b*</u> **5.** and so forth

<u>*d*</u> **6.** versus

<u>*c*</u> **7.** each

a. km

b. etc.

c. ea.

d. vs.

e. lb

f. M.D.

g. qt.

Next Step: Write an imaginary address in a sentence. Use several abbreviations.

Plurals 1

The plurals of most nouns are formed by adding *s* to the singular.

desk – desks   **car – cars**

The plural form of nouns ending in *sh, ch, x, s,* and *z* is made by adding *es* to the singular.

brush – brushes   **fox – foxes**

■ Words Ending in *o*

The plurals of words ending in *o* with a vowel letter just before the *o* are formed by adding *s*.

radio – radios   **video – videos**

The plurals of words ending in *o* with a consonant letter before the *o* are mostly formed by adding *es*.

echo – echoes   **potato – potatoes**

Exception: Musical terms and words borrowed from Spanish form plurals by adding *s*; consult a dictionary for other words of this type.

solo – solos   **taco – tacos**

Other exceptions include the following: photo – photos; yo-yo – yo-yos.

■ Plurals That Do Not Change

A few words in English can have the same form in the singular and plural.

sheep – sheep   **deer – deer**   **trout – trout**

Directions ▶ For each singular word below, write the plural form.

1. suitcase ___*suitcases*___
2. bush ___*bushes*___
3. bee ___*bees*___
4. lunch ___*lunches*___
5. monkey ___*monkeys*___
6. glass ___*glasses*___

7. box ___*boxes*___
8. wish ___*wishes*___
9. toy ___*toys*___
10. moose ___*moose*___
11. rodeo ___*rodeos*___
12. sheep ___*sheep*___

Next Step: Write a brief paragraph of four to five sentences in which you use two or three of the plural nouns above. Write "P" above all the plural nouns you use. Exchange papers with a partner, and check each other's plural spellings.

Plurals 2

The basic rules for forming plurals are listed in the previous activity and in the "Proofreader's Guide." Here are a few additional rules:

- **Words Ending in *ful***

    The plurals of nouns that end with *ful* are formed by adding an *s* at the end of the word.

    spoonful – spoonfuls

- **Words Ending in *f* or *fe***

    The plurals of nouns that end in *f* or *fe* are formed in one of two ways: If the final *f* sound is still heard in the plural form of the word, simply add *s*.

    chief – chiefs

    If the final sound is a *v* sound, change the *f* to *v* and add *es*.

    life – lives

- **Irregular Spelling**

    Some words take on an irregular spelling to form a plural.

    foot – feet   **tooth – teeth**   **goose – geese**

Directions ▶ For each singular word listed below, write the plural form.

1. boy ___*boys*___
2. cave ___*caves*___
3. goose ___*geese*___
4. handful ___*handfuls*___
5. knife ___*knives*___
6. child ___*children*___
7. hoof ___*hooves*___

8. cupful ___*cupfuls*___
9. roof ___*roofs*___
10. video ___*videos*___
11. taco ___*tacos*___
12. trout ___*trout*___
13. calf ___*calves*___
14. wind ___*winds*___

Next Step: Write sentences using the plural forms for each of these words: *mouse, woman, branch,* and *town*. Exchange your work with a classmate and check each other's plurals. *Special Challenge:* Write one sentence that contains the plural forms of all four words.

Numbers

You must learn how to use numbers in your writing. In general, write numbers under 10 as words—*one, two, three,* and so on—and numbers 10 and above as numerals—*10, 15, 75.* But always use numerals in dates and addresses.

■ **Numerals Only**

Use numerals for any numbers in the following forms:

$5.10 (money)   **Highway 45** (identification numbers)

May 10, 2002 (dates)   **555-328-8641** (phone numbers)

756 Dodge Ave. (addresses)   **60303** (ZIP codes)

Directions ⟩ In the following sentences, all the numbers are written as words. Change the words to numerals if appropriate. The first sentence has been done for you.

1. I volunteer at an animal shelter at Highway ~~thirty-three~~ *33* and Wolcott Street.

2. Last week the shelter had ~~thirty-six~~ *36* cats and ~~fifty-three~~ *53* dogs.

3. On May ~~fourteenth, two thousand two~~ *14 2002*, the shelter held an adoption day.

4. On that day, we took ~~twenty-nine~~ *29* cats and ~~twenty~~ *20* dogs to the mall.

5. We hoped that people would adopt at least ~~forty~~ *40* of the animals.

6. I already have three cats at home.

7. My friend has a dog and ~~fifteen~~ *15* tropical fish.

8. It costs only ~~thirty-two dollars~~ *$32* to adopt a pet.

9. That price includes all the animal's shots and a two-week supply of food.

10. For more information about pets, call ~~five five five-three six nine seven~~ *555-3697*.

11. Ask for Ms. Rollin at extension ~~eight fourteen~~ *814*.

12. Write to Adopt-A-Pet, ~~seventeen-hundred~~ *1700* Lynn Avenue, Tula, UT 84001.

Next Step: Write five sentences about going shopping. Include a date, an address, an amount of money, and two or three other numbers of your choice. Exchange your sentences with a classmate and check the use of numbers in each other's work.

Mechanics Review

This activity reviews the rules for using capital letters and numbers.

Directions > Correct any errors in the sentences below. The first sentence has been done for you.

1. One of the greatest ~~a~~(A)merican athletes ever was ~~j~~(J)im ~~t~~(T)horpe.

2. He was born in ~~p~~(P)rague, ~~o~~(O)klahoma, in ~~eighteen eighty-six~~ (1886).

3. Thorpe was a ~~n~~(N)ative ~~a~~(A)merican belonging to the ~~s~~(S)auk and ~~f~~(F)ox tribes.

4. Originally the ~~s~~(S)auk and ~~f~~(F)ox tribes lived around the ~~g~~(G)reat Lakes.

5. As ~~e~~(E)uropeans settled that area, the ~~T~~(t)ribes moved ~~S~~(s)outh toward ~~o~~(O)klahoma.

6. Jim ~~t~~(T)horpe's ~~M~~(m)other, a member of the ~~s~~(S)auk tribe, named him ~~b~~(B)right ~~p~~(P)ath.

7. As a ~~S~~(s)tudent, he played football at ~~c~~(C)arlisle Institute.

8. ~~i~~(I)n ~~nineteen eleven~~ (1911), he led his ~~T~~(t)eam to surprising victories over ~~h~~(H)arvard and ~~a~~(A)rmy.

9. In ~~nineteen twelve~~ (1912), ~~t~~(T)horpe won several ~~M~~(m)edals in ~~T~~(t)he ~~o~~(O)lympics in ~~s~~(S)weden.

10. He won several races and was ~~R~~(r)unner-up in the pentathlon.

11. Later it was discovered that he had played ~~S~~(s)emi-~~P~~(p)rofessional ~~B~~(b)aseball in the ~~n~~(N)orth ~~c~~(C)arolina ~~e~~(E)astern League.

12. Unfortunately, Jim ~~t~~(T)horpe had to return his ~~A~~(a)wards because professional players couldn't compete in the ~~o~~(O)lympics.

13. He later played professional ~~F~~(f)ootball with the ~~c~~(C)hicago Cardinals.

14. Thorpe was one of the ~~F~~(f)irst players admitted to the ~~f~~(F)ootball ~~h~~(H)all of Fame.

15. The ~~M~~(m)ovie ~~j~~(J)im ~~t~~(T)horpe, ~~a~~(A)ll-American made him famous.

Using the Right Word 1

Proofreader's Guide
166-174

Here are some easily confused words. Some words just have one letter that is different.

Whalen was glad to **meet** his new neighbors.
We'll have **meat** and potatoes for dinner.

Benny liked his **new** game.
Salaam **knew** the fastest route.

Four girls ate lunch together.
He bought the watch **for** Joan.

She bruised her **heel.**
The bruise will **heal.**

Our bus was late.
I slept for an **hour.**

Reg was faster **than** Al.
Lil walked and **then** ran.

> **Directions** ▶ If the underlined word is correct, do not change it. If it is incorrect, draw a line through it and write the correct word above it.

1   Everyone had heard about the ~~knew~~ *new* supermarket. There would be at

2   least 15 lanes for checking out. The ~~meet~~ *meat* department would feature some of

3   the best cuts available. People were pleased when they ~~new~~ *knew* there would be

4   fresh fish as well. Our neighbors had never seen such a store. The new

5   place would be two times larger ~~then~~ *than* the old store.

6   While watching the wrecking crew pull down the old store, Angi

7   stepped on a nail and cut her ~~heal~~ *heel*. An ~~our~~ *hour* later she was in the doctor's

8   office so he could clean and bandage the wound. He told her not to put full

9   weight on her foot for three or four days. She listened politely to his

10 suggestions, and ~~than~~ *then* she went to read at the library for an ~~our~~ *hour* or two.

11 She thought she might ~~meat~~ *meet* some of her friends there.

Next Step: Write new sentences for two of the word pairs listed above. Take turns reading your sentences out loud for a partner. Ask your partner to spell the commonly misused word used in each sentence.

Using the Right Word 2

Here are some easily confused words. Some words sound the same, like *miner* and *minor*, but they have different spellings and meanings.

Red is the color of most fire engines.
Abram **read** the book last month.

The **miner** dug for gold.
The rock was only a **minor** problem.

Carefully **pour** some milk in that glass.
Some cars are **poor** quality.

Mercury is a heavy **metal**.
Bri won a **medal** in the race.

The cut caused him **pain**.
The bird hit a **pane** in the window.

Francine likes a **quiet** room.
Joseph **quit** that job last year.
It's **quite** easy for him.

Directions ❯ In the following sentences, look at the underlined words. If a word is correct, do not change it. If it is incorrect, cross out the word and write the correct word above it.

1. Only a few Olympic athletes win more than one ~~metal~~. *medal*

2. The student claimed he had <u>read</u> the book and seen the movie.

3. Some people are ~~pour~~, while others are rich. *poor*

4. The library rules state that students must be ~~quite~~ while they study. *quiet*

5. The dent in the refrigerator was ~~miner~~. *minor*

6. A small paper cut can be a real <u>pain</u>.

7. Steel is a strong <u>metal</u> used in buildings and bridges.

8. The book cover is a bright shade of ~~read~~. *red*

9. The boys were told to ~~quite~~ making noise. *quit*

10. Coal <u>miners</u> do dangerous work.

Next Step: On your own paper, use the following word pairs in sentences: "hole" and "whole"; "brake" and "break." Write one sentence for each pair.

Using the Right Word 3

Proofreader's Guide 166-174

Here are some easily confused words. Some words look similar, such as *desert* and *dessert*, but they are pronounced differently.

The girls closed **their** books.
The gym is over **there**.

I have **one** pencil.
Venus Williams **won** her tennis match.

The **desert** is a very dry place.
The **dessert** was ice cream.

A **bear** is a large animal.
The sun will burn **bare** skin.

Dena has **some** flowers.
The **sum** of 22 and 23 is 45.

Move over **so** I can fit in.
Anne learned to **sew** a dress.

Directions ▶ If the underlined word is correct, do not change it. If it is incorrect, cross out the word and write the correct word above it.

1. Frena said the sand in the ~~dessert~~ *desert* was hot.

2. Jermaine stopped at the store to buy ~~won~~ *one* book.

3. David tried to ~~so~~ *sew* a button on his shirt.

4. The <u>sum</u> of three plus six is nine.

5. The custodian picked up the snake with his ~~bear~~ *bare* hand.

6. ~~Their~~ *There* are five statues in the city park.

7. He went <u>so</u> close to the fire he burned his face.

8. José easily ~~one~~ *won* the writing contest.

9. <u>Some</u> people stood by the door; they wanted to see <u>their</u> scores.

10. Hal could not finish ~~sum~~ *some* of his <u>dessert</u>.

11. How much does a grizzly ~~bare~~ *bear* weigh?

Next Step: On your own paper, write a paragraph about a memorable dessert that correctly uses some of the words listed above. Have a partner check your paragraph for correct usage of these words.

Using the Right Word 4

There are many words that are commonly confused and used incorrectly. For example, *its* is confused with *it's*, and *leave* is sometimes confused with *let*.

It's a warm day today.
Its edge is sharp.

Today's **weather** is nice.
I don't know **whether** I should go.

I feel this is the **right** time to begin.
I will **write** a letter tomorrow.

I hope to **hear** the concert tonight.
Suzanne came **here** on Tuesday.

He doesn't **know** the difference.
She found **no** peanut butter.

I am too **weak** to lift that stone.
Next **week** I will begin my job.

I would like that game, **too**.
I have **two** bike tires.
He went **to** school today.

Celine must **wait** for the bus.
Tai checked his **weight**.

Directions ▶ Read this story as a class. Did the writer use the underlined words correctly? Cross out any incorrect word and write the correct word above it. The first one has been done for you.

1   The ~~whether~~ *weather* will be quite stormy <u>hear</u> *here* today. That is ~~know~~ *no* surprise.

2   ~~Its~~ *It's* supposed <u>too</u> *to* get very hot and then turn cold. Conditions will be just

3   right for lightning, thunder, and rain. There is a chance for hail, <u>two</u> *too*. Last

4   <u>weak</u> *week* was great baseball ~~whether~~ *weather*. I suppose bad <u>weather</u> will be okay,

5   because I have to ~~right~~ *write* a report for my science class. The subject will be

6   horses. The teacher said the whole class would want to ~~here~~ *hear* it. She likes

7   horses, <u>too</u>, and can hardly ~~weight~~ *wait* to <u>hear</u> what I have <u>too</u> *to* say. She wants

8   to ~~no~~ *know* all she can about these incredible animals. I don't think anyone likes

9   horses as much as she does.

Next Step: On your own paper, use the following word pair in a sentence—"learn" and "teach."

Using the Right Word Review

This exercise reviews the easily confused words that you have studied.

Directions >> Read the following sentences. If an underlined word is used incorrectly, cross it out and write the correct word above it.

1. The ~~whether~~ *weather* was perfect for the soccer game.

2. Last ~~weak~~ *week* the coach had announced that I would be the goalie.

3. His quiet confidence encouraged me, and I easily stopped ~~for~~ *four* powerful shots.

4. Our opponent ~~new~~ *knew* this was the game of the year.

5. As the match continued, ~~there~~ *their* defense grew ~~week~~ *weak*.

6. Finally ~~to~~ *two* of ~~hour~~ *our* players slipped in and scored a goal.

7. The score was 1-0, with ~~too~~ *two* minutes to go.

8. ~~Than~~ *Then* it happened—some near-perfect passes started the breakaway.

9. There was no one ~~two~~ *to* stop him but me.

10. I could ~~here~~ *hear* the crowd roar, and my ~~bear~~ *bare* skin tingled.

11. "Don't wait ~~two~~ *too* long. Go out and meet him on your terms," I said to myself.

12. "~~Its~~ *It's* okay. You know you can do this!"

13. I was nervous, ~~sew~~ *so* I focused on the red and white soccer ball.

14. He broke to the right and let the ball get too far ahead.

15. It was a ~~miner~~ *minor* mistake, but I took ~~too~~ *two* quick strides and dove ~~four~~ *for* the ball.

16. Our team defeated the district champs, and I ~~one~~ *won* MVP.

Sentence Activities

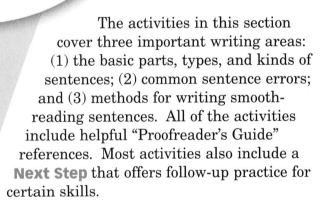

The activities in this section cover three important writing areas: (1) the basic parts, types, and kinds of sentences; (2) common sentence errors; and (3) methods for writing smooth-reading sentences. All of the activities include helpful "Proofreader's Guide" references. Most activities also include a **Next Step** that offers follow-up practice for certain skills.

Basic Sentence Patterns

Sentences in the English language follow these basic patterns:

■ **Subject + Action Verb**

    S   AV
Georgina runs. (The action verb "runs" is intransitive. It does not need a direct object to express a complete thought.)

■ **Subject + Action Verb + Direct Object**

    S   AV   DO
Franklin throws the ball. (The action verb "throws" is transitive. It does need a direct object to express a complete thought.)

■ **Subject + Action Verb + Indirect Object + Direct Object**

   S   AV   IO   DO
Lana gave her friend a quarter. (The indirect object "friend" receives the action of the verb, indirectly. It names the person *to whom* or *for whom* something is done.)

■ **Subject + Action Verb + Direct Object + Object Complement**

     S   AV   DO   OC
The team voted Ricardo the best linebacker. (The object complement "linebacker" renames or describes the direct object "Ricardo.")

■ **Subject + Linking Verb + Predicate Noun**

    S LV   PN
Suann is a very nice person. (The linking verb "is" joins one idea to another. The predicate noun "person" renames the subject "Suann.")

■ **Subject + Linking Verb + Predicate Adjective**

     S LV PA
The boy is funny. (The predicate adjective "funny" follows the linking verb "is" and modifies the subject "boy.")

> **Directions** > Write two original sentences for each of the basic patterns.

1. Subject + Action Verb

The coyote howled.

Bella laughs.

2. Subject + Action Verb + Direct Object

Erica rode the crosstown bus.

Eric strummed the guitar.

3. Subject + Action Verb + Indirect Object + Direct Object

My friend gave me a birthday card.

Joe's parents bought him an old car.

4. Subject + Action Verb + Direct Object + Object Complement

Johan named his dog Scout.

Conda calls Viola her best friend.

5. Subject + Linking Verb + Predicate Noun

A mare is a female horse.

The train is enjoyable transportation.

6. Subject + Linking Verb + Predicate Adjective

The tree stump looked scary.

The girl is smart.

Next Step: Pick four of the sentence forms from the list on page 47. On a separate sheet of paper, write a different sentence for each form. Then exchange papers with a classmate and label each other's sentences (S AV; S AV DO; and so on).

Simple Subjects and Predicates 1

Every complete sentence has a subject and a predicate (verb) and expresses a complete thought. The **simple subject** is either a noun (*Mr. Heller, backpack*) or a pronoun (*he, she, we, they,* and so on). The **simple predicate** is either an action verb (*grow, laugh*) or a linking verb (*is, are, was, were,* and so on).

A <u>tree</u> <u><u>provides</u></u> shade on warm days.
("Tree" is the simple subject; "provides" is the simple predicate.)

<u>Trees</u> <u><u>are</u></u> sturdy plants.
("Trees" is the simple subject; "are" is the simple predicate.)

Directions ▶ In the sentences below, underline the simple subject with one line; underline the simple predicate with two lines. The first sentence has been done for you.

1. <u>Leaves</u> on trees <u><u>grow</u></u> at different times of the year.

2. <u>Trees</u> <u><u>need</u></u> air, food, water, and sunlight.

3. A <u>tree</u> <u><u>has</u></u> roots, a trunk, limbs, and branches.

4. The <u>roots</u> of most trees <u><u>lie</u></u> under the ground.

5. <u>They</u> often <u><u>spread</u></u> in many directions, even under sidewalks.

6. <u>Trees</u> <u><u>are</u></u> the oldest living things on earth.

7. <u>Trees</u> <u><u>grow</u></u> in almost any weather condition, in deserts, and on mountains.

8. <u>Willows</u> often <u><u>grow</u></u> near water.

9. <u>We</u> <u><u>get</u></u> many useful products from trees.

10. Most wooden <u>furniture</u> <u><u>comes</u></u> from tree trunks.

11. Many <u>birds</u> <u><u>build</u></u> nests in trees.

Next Step: Write five sentences about the trees in your neighborhood or a nearby park. Underline your simple subjects once and your simple predicates twice.

Simple Subjects and Predicates 2

All sentences have subjects and predicates. A simple subject is the subject without any words describing or modifying it. A simple predicate is the verb without any words modifying or completing it.

Henry sleeps in the sun.

Our old cat was more active.

> **Directions** In each sentence below, underline each simple subject once and each simple predicate twice. The first sentence has been done for you.

1. Aaron saw the show.

2. Angela's uncle is a teacher.

3. The two friends walk to school together.

4. I ran up the stairs.

5. We visit my grandfather every week.

6. Hungrily, the striped cat drank the milk.

7. Ramon found his sneakers under the bed.

8. Maria divides her time between homework and basketball practice.

9. Anna won the trophy for best science project.

10. My dog, a beagle, chewed the curtains in the living room.

11. He also scratched the front door.

12. Hot and tired, we walked home.

13. Throughout the night, the thunder roared.

Next Step: Write a short paragraph about what you like to do during the summer. Then exchange papers with a classmate. Underline all the simple subjects once and the simple predicates twice.

Compound Subjects and Predicates 1

Sentences may have compound subjects or compound predicates (verbs). Some sentences may have both. A **compound subject** has more than one simple subject connected by *and* or *or*. Likewise a **compound predicate** has more than one simple predicate connected by *and, but,* or *or.*

Green and purple are my favorite colors.
(The subject "green" and "purple" is compound.)

I paint or draw to relax.
(The verb "paint" and "draw" is compound.)

My sister and brother like panting but hate cleaning up.
(The subject and verb are both compound.)

 **Directions** In the following sentences, underline the simple subject once and the simple predicate twice. The subjects and predicates in the sentences may or may not be compound. The first sentence has been done for you.

1. Art or music is my favorite subject.

2. My brother and sister prefer science.

3. They like all rocks but look only for certain kinds in the park.

4. I stay at home and paint.

5. My colored pencils or paints are always handy.

6. My friend and I often go to the park, too.

7. Sometimes Yolanda and I meet my brother and sister after school.

8. They review our sketches or study our designs.

9. Then they open their bags and show us their rocks.

10. Some of the rocks have unusual shapes.

Next Step: Find a brief newspaper or magazine article. Identify all the compound subjects and predicates by underlining the subjects once and the predicates twice.

Compound Subjects and Predicates 2

Sentences may have compound subjects or compound predicates. Some sentences may have both.

Directions ▶ For each sentence, supply the missing compound subject or compound predicate. Write your answers on the blank lines. The first sentence has been done for you.

Answers will vary.

1. __Saturday__ and __Sunday__ always pass quickly. *(compound subject)*

2. The waiter __brought__ us water and __took__ our orders. *(compound predicate)*

3. Both __Jill__ and __Taio__ play the drums. *(compound subject)*

4. At home __Mom__ and __Dad__ speak Spanish. *(compound subject)*

5. My __brother__ and __sister__ always attend at least one baseball game each season. *(compound subject)*

6. Last summer my __family__ and __I__ went camping. *(compound subject)*

7. They __caught__ fish, __cooked__ them, and __ate__ them for dinner. *(compound predicate)*

8. Two __boys__ and three __girls__ were in line ahead of me. *(compound subject)*

9. At the corner market we __chose__ fresh fruits and vegetables and __placed__ them in a wicker basket. *(compound predicate)*

10. My __friend__ and __I__ like that store. *(compound subject)*

Next Step: Write two sentences that use both a compound subject and a compound predicate.

Types of Sentences 1

There are three basic types of sentences: simple, compound, and complex.

- ### Simple Sentence

    A simple sentence has a subject and a verb.

    My mother is a nurse.

    (This simple sentence has one subject, "mother," and one verb, "is.")

    She advises and treats many people.

    (This simple sentence has one subject,"she," and a compound verb, "advises" and "treats.")

    My mother and my aunt work together.

    (This simple sentence has a compound subject, "mother" and "aunt," and one verb, "work.")

- ### Compound Sentence

    A compound sentence has at least two simple sentences (also called independent clauses) joined by a comma and a coordinating conjunction.

    Mom works in the emergency room, but she also works in the recovery room.

    (This compound sentence is joined by a comma and "but.")

- ### Complex Sentence

    A complex sentence has one or more dependent clause and only one independent clause.

    After Mom finishes work, she works out at the fitness center.

    (This complex sentence has one dependent clause, "after Mom finishes work," and one independent clause, "she works out at the fitness center.")

 **Identify each of the following sentences by writing "simple," "compound," or "complex" in the blank space. The first sentence has been done for you.**

simple   **1.** Florence Nightingale influenced modern health care.

complex   **2.** Even when she was a young girl, this future nurse was

interested in health.

simple   **3.** Florence Nightingale was born in Italy in 1820.

compound   **4.** Her family was wealthy, and they provided Florence with many toys and games.

complex   **5.** Her favorite game was to pretend her dolls were ill because then she could help them.

compound   **6.** She always wanted to help people, and she knew about the poor conditions in hospitals at that time.

simple   **7.** In the nineteenth century, young women usually had no profession.

complex   **8.** Although her family was against it, she studied health and became a nurse.

complex   **9.** When she heard about terrible conditions in military hospitals, she sailed to Turkey during the Crimean War.

simple   **10.** She took 38 other dedicated nurses with her to help the wounded soldiers.

complex   **11.** Because she stayed up at night caring for the soldiers, she always carried a lantern.

simple   **12.** She became known as the Lady with the Lamp.

compound   **13.** Florence Nightingale never stopped trying to improve health care, and the soldiers loved and respected her for her efforts.

complex   **14.** Although her own health suffered because of her work, Florence Nightingale lived to be 90 years old.

Next Step: Write a simple sentence, a compound sentence, and a complex sentence about a health-related topic: an illness or injury, a doctor or nurse you know, and so on. Read your sentences to the class.

Types of Sentences 2

Proofreader's Guide
176, 186

There are three basic types of sentences: simple, compound, and complex.

■ **Simple Sentence**

<u>Sarah</u> <u>bought</u> hot lunch.
(This simple sentence has one subject, "Sarah," and one verb, "bought.")

■ **Compound Sentence**

<u>Sarah</u> <u>bought</u> hot lunch, but <u>Josie</u> <u>brought</u> her own.
(This compound sentence is joined by a comma and "but.")

■ **Complex Sentence**

<u>Sarah</u> <u>bought</u> hot lunch because the daily <u>special</u> <u>was</u> roasted chicken.
(This complex sentence has one dependent clause, "because the daily special was roasted chicken," and one independent clause, "Sarah bought hot lunch.")

> **Directions** Rewrite each of the following simple sentences. First, create a compound sentence by adding an independent clause (another simple sentence). Then, create a complex sentence by adding a dependent clause. Use the connecting word given in parentheses. The first one has been done for you.

Answers will vary.

1. Hans will sing in the talent show.

   compound: *(and)* _Hans will sing in the talent show, and I will play the piano._

   complex: *(if)* _Hans will sing in the talent show if I play the piano for him._

2. My brother loves rap music.

   compound: *(and)* _My brother loves rap music, and he buys many rap CD's._

   complex: *(because)* _My brother loves rap music because he likes the rhythm._

3. My grandfather likes to cook.

compound: *(but)* _My grandfather likes to cook, but he does not like to wash the dishes._

complex: *(when)* _My grandfather likes to cook when people are hungry._

4. I read the whole book.

compound: *(and)* _I read the whole book, and I enjoyed the story very much._

complex: *(before)* _I read the whole book before I went to school._

5. Luann rides her bike to school.

compound: *(and)* _Luann rides her bike to school, and her friends usually ride with her._

complex: *(if)* _Luann rides her bike to school if it's not raining._

6. Jermaine plays basketball.

compound: *(but)* _Jermaine plays basketball, but he likes football, too._

complex: *(when)* _Jermaine plays basketball when he has time._

Next Step: Rewrite the compound and complex sentences in sentences 5 and 6 above using different connecting words.

Kinds of Sentences 1

There are four kinds of sentences:

- **Declarative** (makes a statement)
  My aunt and uncle live downtown.

- **Interrogative** (asks a question)
  Do they live near the sports center?

- **Imperative** (gives a command)
  Take the train to their house.

- **Exclamatory** (shows strong emotion or surprise)
  You won't believe how much traffic there is!

Directions ▶ Label each sentence below as "declarative," "interrogative," "imperative," or "exclamatory." Then add the correct end punctuation mark. The first one has been done for you.

interrogative   **1.** Has your elevator ever been broken?

declarative   **2.** Our elevator has been broken since Monday.

declarative   **3.** I climb nine flights of stairs to get to our apartment.

exclamatory   **4.** Wow, was I ever tired!

declarative   **5.** That climb took forever.

declarative   **6.** Someone left a note on the elevator door.

imperative   **7.** "See the superintendent before turning off the electricity."

declarative   **8.** I guess this note is for the repair people.

interrogative   **9.** Will they fix the elevator tomorrow?

exclamatory   **10.** Man, I hope so!

Next Step: Write a paragraph (or two) about a good or bad day. Be sure to use one declarative sentence, one interrogative sentence, one imperative sentence, and one exclamatory sentence.

Kinds of Sentences 2

There are four kinds of sentences:

■ **Declarative** (makes a statement)

Clarinets and violins are both musical instruments.

■ **Interrogative** (asks a question)

Which of these is a wind instrument?

■ **Imperative** (gives a command)

Turn down your radio.

■ **Exclamatory** (shows strong emotion or surprise)

I just love beautiful music!

> **Directions** ⟩ Think about the music that you enjoy listening to or playing. On the lines below, write two sentences of each kind about your favorite music. *Answers will vary.*

1. Declarative *I enjoy popular music.*

I listen to music at least four hours a day.

_____

2. Interrogative *Do you like popular music, or do you prefer country music?*

Are you going to buy their latest CD?

_____

3. Imperative *Listen to this song.*

Please turn the volume up.

_____

4. Exclamatory *That's the greatest concert I've ever heard!*

Wow, is that drummer good!

_____

Sentence Fragments 1

A **sentence fragment** is a type of sentence error that occurs when a group of words is missing a subject, a verb, or both.

Fragment: **Went to the library.**
(The subject is missing.)

Corrected: **Aiden went to the library.**
(The subject "Aiden" is added.)

Fragment: **Most people in my building.**
(The verb is missing.)

Corrected: **Most people in my building use the laundry room.**
(The verb "use" is added.)

Fragment: **Always in use in the gym.**
(Both the subject and verb are missing.)

Corrected **The treadmill is always in use in the gym.**
(The subject "treadmill" and the verb "is" are added.)

Directions Write "S" for sentence on the line if the group of words expresses a complete thought. Write "F" for fragment if the group of words does not express a complete thought.

Corrections will vary.

_S_ **1.** Exercise is good for people.

_F_ **2.** *I lift weights* Four hours a week.

_F_ **3.** The stair climber and rowing machine *work different muscles.*

_S_ **4.** I enjoy exercising.

_F_ **5.** *Biking for one and a half hours* Can burn about 250 calories.

_S_ **6.** Weights strengthen individual muscles.

_F_ **7.** Some people in their teens *need to exercise more*

_F_ **8.** After 30 minutes of lifting, *I feel great*

Directions Write a complete sentence for each fragment in the exercise above. Use your own paper and share your new sentences with a classmate.

Write "S" before each group of words that expresses a complete thought. Write "F" before each fragment. Then correct each fragment. The first one has been done for you.

The word thermometer comes

F **1.** ⌃From the Greek words *thermo* meaning "heat" and *meter* meaning "measure."

S **2.** We use a thermometer to measure temperature.

F **3.** A thermometer ⌃*is* a small glass tube with a bulb at the end.

F **4.** The tube ⌃*is* filled with mercury.

S **5.** Heat makes the mercury rise.

S **6.** As the temperature goes higher, the mercury rises.

F **7.** *There are* ⌃Two main ways to measure temperature.

F **8.** Fahrenheit ⌃*is used* in the United States, and Celsius is used in European countries.

S **9.** Celsius is also known as centigrade.

S **10.** On the Fahrenheit scale, water freezes at 32 degrees.

F **11.** On the Celsius scale ⌃*water freezes* at zero.

S **12.** The normal body temperature is 98.6 degrees Fahrenheit.

S **13.** Most people are comfortable when the temperature is about 72 degrees.

F **14.** Very cold temperatures ⌃*can be dangerous*

S **15.** The Fahrenheit scale measures temperature in smaller increments (degrees) than the Celsius scale does.

Next Step: Using the information above, write a paragraph explaining the difference between Fahrenheit and Celsius. Share your work with a classmate.

Sentence Fragments 2

A sentence fragment is a common sentence error that expresses an incomplete idea because it is missing a subject, verb, or both.

Fragment: **Ate in a hurry.** (The subject is missing.)
Corrected: **He ate in a hurry.**

Fragment: **Dangerous snow-covered steps.** (The verb is missing.)
Corrected: **Snow-covered steps are dangerous.**

Fragment: **Never easy for me.** (The subject and verb are missing.)
Corrected: **Running is never easy for me.**

Directions ⟩ Before each group of words, write "S" if it is a sentence and "F" if it is a fragment. For each fragment, decide what is missing—the subject, verb, or both—and write that word on the second line. The first sentence has been done for you.

Corrections will vary.

__F__ **1.** One famous abolitionist _{was} Sojourner Truth. ____*verb*____

__S__ **2.** Isabella Hardenburgh was her real name. _____

__F__ **3.** _{She} Was born into slavery. ____*subject*____

__F__ **4.** She and her family _{lived} in Ulster County, New York. ____*verb*____

__F__ **5.** _{Isabella} Thought Sojourner Truth was a better name. ____*subject*____

__S__ **6.** She traveled around the country to speak the truth. _____

__F__ **7.** _{She} Opposed slavery and supported women's rights. ____*subject*____

__F__ **8.** "Ain't I a Woman?" _{was} her famous speech. ____*verb*____

__S__ **9.** Sojourner Truth said that women were as strong as men. _____

__F__ **10.** _{She} Spent time in Washington, D.C. ____*subject*____

__F__ **11.** _{Sojourner} Wanted to improve conditions for African Americans. ____*subject*____

__F__ **12.** The year of her death _{was} 1883. ____*verb*____

Next Step: Correct each fragment and share your corrected sentences with a classmate.

Sentence Fragments 3

A sentence fragment is a common sentence error in which a group of words fails to express a complete idea. The fragment may be missing a subject, a verb, or both.

Fragment: **Onions for Mom's special chili.**
(The subject and the verb are missing.)

Corrected: **I chopped onions for Mom's special chili.**
(The subject "I" and the verb "chopped" have been added.)

Directions Write "S" on the first line if the group of words is a complete sentence. Write "F" if it is a fragment. For each fragment, decide what is missing—the subject, the verb, or both. Write "subject," "verb," or "both" on the line at the end of the sentence. The first one has been done for you.

Corrections will vary.

___F___ 1. ^We^ Went to the store for milk and eggs. ___subject___

___S___ 2. Do not shop when you are hungry. _____

___F___ 3. ^We^ Forgot to bring the shopping list. ___subject___

___F___ 4. The store ^was^ out of ground turkey. ___verb___

___F___ 5. ^We^ Selected chicken wings instead. ___subject___

___S___ 6. It is important to compare prices. _____

___F___ 7. ^There was^ No bottled barbecue sauce like ours. ___verb (or) both___

___F___ 8. ^We^ Wanted to make a chili recipe. ___subject___

___S___ 9. We needed more hot chili peppers. _____

___F___ 10. We always ^buy^ potato chips. ___verb___

___F___ 11. Shopping ^is^ easy when lines are short. ___verb___

Next Step: Turn the fragments in this exercise into complete sentences by adding an appropriate subject, verb, or both to each one. Compare your results with a classmate's.

Run-On Sentences 1

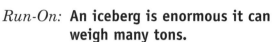

A **run-on sentence** has two sentences joined without punctuation or without a comma and a coordinating conjunction (*and, or, for, but, nor, yet,* and *so*).

Run-On: **An iceberg is enormous it can weigh many tons.**
(No punctuation or connecting word joins these two sentences.)

Corrected: **An iceberg is enormous. It can weigh many tons.**
(A period is placed between the two sentences. Begin the new sentence with a capital letter.)

An iceberg is enormous; it can weigh many tons.
(A semicolon separates the two sentences.)

An iceberg is enormous, so it can weigh many tons.
(A comma and the conjunction "so" connect the two sentences.)

> **Directions**

If the group of words is a run-on sentence, write "RO" on the line. If the words form a correct sentence, write "S." Add necessary punctuation to correct the run-on sentences. the first one has been done for you.   *Corrections may vary.*

RO 1. Water has three forms$_\wedge$ they are liquid, solid, and gas.
      $;$

RO 2. Water from a tap is liquid. steam from boiling water is gas.
      $\overset{S}{/}$

S 3. Ice is water in its frozen or solid form.

RO 4. Ice is less dense than water is$_\wedge$ that's why it floats.
      $;$

S 5. Ice melts at 33 degrees Fahrenheit.

S 6. Ice can evaporate without melting.

RO 7. Water boils at or above 212 degrees Fahrenheit$_\wedge$ it is hot enough to
      $;$
      cause third-degree burns.

S 8. Water boils at a lower temperature on high mountains.

> **Directions**

Share your answers with the class or with a small group. Talk about different ways to correct these run-on sentences.

_RO_ **1.** Ice is lighter than water $\overset{so}{\wedge}$ it floats.

_S_ **2.** Put an ice cube in a glass of water, and the cube will float.

_S_ **3.** Notice most of the ice in the glass is underwater.

_RO_ **4.** An iceberg is similar to the ice cube in the glass of water $\overset{;}{\wedge}$ most of it lies underwater.

_S_ **5.** Only a small part is visible above the waterline.

_RO_ **6.** Icebergs and ice cubes both float. $\overset{T}{\text{they}}$ are similar in another way.

_S_ **7.** Both consist of water crystals.

_RO_ **8.** However, there is one big difference $\overset{;}{\wedge}$ $\overset{A}{\text{an}}$ iceberg begins as snow.

_RO_ **9.** Snow is water vapor that has frozen. $\overset{A}{\text{a}}$ snowflake is a frozen water crystal.

_S_ **10.** Snow hardens when it sits on the ground for a long time.

_S_ **11.** Icebergs and glaciers form from hardened snow.

_RO_ **12.** More snow adds weight $\overset{and}{\wedge}$ the ice becomes very hard.

_S_ **13.** Most icebergs are actually pieces of a glacier.

_RO_ **14.** Water is amazing $\overset{;}{\wedge}$ it can appear in so many shapes and forms.

Next Step: Correct the run-on sentences in the sentences above. Compare your corrections with a classmate's.

Run-On Sentences 2

Remember, two sentences joined without punctuation or a comma and a coordinating conjunction create a sentence error called a run-on sentence. Some common conjunctions are *and, or, for, but, nor, so,* and *yet.*

Run-On: **There are many kinds of squirrels gray squirrels are the most common.**

Corrected: **There are many kinds of squirrels. Gray squirrels are the most common.** (A period is placed between the two sentences. Begin the new sentence with a capital letter.)

There are many kinds of squirrels; gray squirrels are the most common. (A semicolon separates the two sentences.)

There are many kinds of squirrels, but gray squirrels are the most common. (A comma and the connecting word "but" connect the two sentences.)

Directions ▶ Write "RO" on the line if the group of words is a run-on sentence. Use correct capitalization and punctuation to divide each run-on into two sentences. If the sentence is correct, write "S" on the line. The first one has been done for you.

_RO_ **1.** Gray squirrels are often found in town. They build nests in trees.

_S_ **2.** Another kind of squirrel is the tuft-eared squirrel.

_RO_ **3.** Tuft-eared squirrels live in the Southwest. They are larger than gray squirrels.

_RO_ **4.** Kaibob squirrels are a kind of tuft-eared squirrel. These squirrels have completely white tails.

_RO_ **5.** Flying squirrels don't really fly. Their movements just make it look like they are flying.

_S_ **6.** The skin attached to their legs looks like wings.

_RO_ **7.** Flying squirrels jump and glide through the air. They seem to fly.

Next Step: Now correct each run-on sentence above in another way. Use a comma and a conjunction (*and, or, so, but,* or *yet*) to create a compound sentence. (See the final example at the top of the page.)

Comma Splices 1

A **comma splice** is an error in which two sentences are incorrectly joined with a comma. An end punctuation mark, a semicolon, or a comma plus a coordinating conjuction like *and, but, yet,* or *so* may be used to correct the comma splice.

Comma Splice: **I will write about cities, I plan to tell how they should change.**
Corrected: **I will write about cities, and I plan to tell how they should change.**
(The connecting word "and" has been added.)

Directions ▶ Write "CS" in front of sentences that have a comma splice. Then correct those sentences by adding a connecting word. If a sentence is correct, write "S" on the line in front of it. The first one has been done for you. *Corrections may vary.*

_CS_ **1.** The earliest cities were built in the Middle East around 4000 B.C.E., ^*and* they were located in the valleys of the Tigris and Euphrates Rivers.

_CS_ **2.** Many villages were well established, ^*but* they didn't become cities until they were larger and supported specialized trades.

_CS_ **3.** Villages housed only farming families, ^*but* cities had families who produced other necessities that they traded for food.

_S_ **4.** That has not changed; people depend on each other in cities.

_CS_ **5.** For example, you don't raise all your vegetables or make all your clothes, ^*and* you don't hammer out your own knives and forks.

_CS_ **6.** City people earn money at work, ^*and* they spend their money to buy what they need from other people.

_CS_ **7.** Some ancient villages were as large as small cities, ^*yet* without specialized craftspeople, administrators, and military leaders, these communities remained villages.

Comma Splices 2

A comma splice occurs when two simple sentences are incorrectly connected with a comma. An end punctuation mark, a semicolon, or a comma *plus* a coordinating conjunction may be used to correct a comma splice. Remember, if you correct a comma splice using end punctuation, you *must* capitalize the first word of the remaining simple sentence.

Comma Splice: **The boys go over to the gym to practice, they also lift weights.**
Corrected: **The boys go over to the gym to practice; they also lift weights.**

Directions ▶ In the sentences below, write "CS" in front of each comma splice and "S" in front of each correct sentence. Correct each comma splice with an end punctuation mark or a semicolon. The first one has been done for you. *Corrections may vary.*

___CS___ **1.** What do you want for lunch, would you like pizza?

___S___ **2.** This place serves vegetarian meals, but I have not tried any.

___CS___ **3.** Cafeteria food is easy and inexpensive, it is quicker than bringing lunch from home.

___CS___ **4.** Maria enjoys a peanut-butter-and-jelly sandwich and an apple, I would rather have a hamburger, fries, and a soda.

___S___ **5.** Rice with vegetables is a popular item on the menu, and homemade apple pie is a local favorite.

___CS___ **6.** My friend brings leftovers from home, they always look better than what is on my tray.

___CS___ **7.** We never have leftovers, my brothers eat everything that gets put on the table.

___CS___ **8.** Some kids bring the same thing for lunch every day, that would be very boring to me.

_CS_ **9.** I got tired of packing my own lunch, making sandwiches every

morning started to get to me.

_CS_ **10.** Our school has an International Week, the menu reflects a

different foreign cuisine each day.

_CS_ **11.** The Chinese menu consists of ginger chicken, beef chow mein, and

steamed rice, everyone loves it.

_CS_ **12.** Thai cuisine is popular, the cooks make it less spicy for us.

_S_ **13.** We like the Italian menu, but it better include pizza and pasta!

_CS_ **14.** Tacos, fajitas, and burritos are on the regular menu, they are

featured on Mexican-food day as well.

_CS_ **15.** Macaroni and cheese, chili, and hamburgers are U.S.A.-menu

favorites, mashed potatoes with gravy are also popular.

_CS_ **16.** Almost everyone wants Korean barbeque on the regular menu, few

people asked for more kim chee (spicy pickled cabbage), however.

_CS_ **17.** Mediterranean pita bread, chicken kabobs, and dolmas (marinated

grape leaves stuffed with rice) surprised us last year, everyone

wondered what the kitchen staff would do next.

_S_ **18.** We should vote on next year's International Week menu; Vanessa

thinks French crepes and omelets would be popular dishes.

Next Step: Write three sentences (two should include a comma splice) about your ideal lunch menu. Exchange your work with a partner. Identify and correct the comma splices.

Sentence Errors Review 1

Think about what you have learned. A **sentence fragment** is a group of words without a subject, a verb, or both. It does not express a complete thought. A **run-on sentence** happens when two sentences are joined without proper punctuation or a comma and a coordinating conjunction.

Proofreader's Guide
178, 186

> **Directions** ▶ Read the groups of words below. Write "RO" in front of the run-on sentences, and "F" in front of the sentence fragments.

Corrections will vary.

RO 1. Tomorrow I'm baby-sitting for my neighbor's little girl ; she is only three years old.

RO 2. It's the first time I'm baby-sitting. I'm taking Dalia to the park.

F 3. _I_ Will watch her in the sandbox.

F 4. _She_ Likes the slide best.

RO 5. Then I'll make her lunch. _S_ she likes cereal with sliced bananas.

RO 6. After lunch she takes a nap , _and_ then I wash the dishes and do some of my homework.

F 7. _Dalia will still be sleeping_ When my neighbor comes back.

RO 8. I think everything will be fine ; I learned first aid in school.

F 9. _I'll dial_ 911 in an emergency.

RO 10. Also, we live one flight down , _and_ my dad will be home.

Next Step: Correct the run-on sentences and sentence fragments above.

Special Challenge: Imagine that you are the child who is being left for the first time with a new baby-sitter. Write how you might feel about the event and about the baby-sitter. Write complete sentences.

Sentence Errors Review 2

This exercise reviews common sentence errors.

Directions ▶ **Each of the following sentences contains an error. Write "F" in front of the fragments, "RO" in front of the run-ons, and "CS" in front of the comma splices. Then correct each error. The first sentence has been done for you.**

Corrections will vary.

<u>CS</u> **1.** Lots of people have an easy time baby-sitting, ~~they~~ *T* they just go to the house and play with the kids.

<u>CS</u> **2.** Then the kids go to sleep, *and* the baby-sitter watches TV.

<u>F</u> **3.** *That* Didn't happen to my sister, though.

<u>RO</u> **4.** She's in high school. I think she used to like baby-sitting.

<u>F</u> **5.** *She* Has done a lot of baby-sitting.

<u>F</u> **6.** But *she baby-sat* never for my cousin's twin boys.

<u>CS</u> **7.** Those twins are terrible, *T* the family has trouble finding baby-sitters.

<u>RO</u> **8.** They fight with each other, *and* they also pick on their older brother.

<u>CS</u> **9.** They often make a mess; they blame it on him.

<u>F</u> **10.** *They* Always say, "We saw him do it!"

<u>CS</u> **11.** The twins often spill milk and juice on the floor, *and* they always throw food.

<u>F</u> **12.** Their dog Ruff *is* the only one who will play with them.

Next Step: Write three sentences about a difficult job you've done. Exchange your sentences with a classmate. Make sure that your partner's sentences are correct.

Rambling Sentences

A **rambling sentence** happens when you put together too many little sentences using *and, but,* and *so*. Avoid rambling sentences in your writing.

Rambling: **Sometimes Frank and Armand like to go downtown to see the lights and all the stores so they take the bus downtown and they walk all around and then they usually find a place to grab some burgers.**
(All the ideas are connected by "and" and "so" in this rambling sentence.)

Corrected: **Sometimes Frank and Armand like to go downtown to see the lights and all the stores. After getting off the bus, they walk all around and usually find a place to grab some burgers.**
(The ideas are now expressed by a simple and a complex sentence.)

Directions ▶ Correct the following rambling sentences. You may cross out some words, and you may change some of the words. Also add capitalization and punctuation as needed.

Corrections will vary.

1. We wanted to play soccer, so we walked over to the park. and found an
                                                              We
   empty field, and we played for three hours.

2. After a while we got very hungry, but we were too far from home to
                                      W
   grab a snack. and we really wanted to keep playing and eat at the
                                 F
   concession stand. so finally we asked a friend to lend us some money.

3. Our friend had just enough money for a couple burgers, so we quickly
                                  T
   ran to buy them. but the concession sold only hot dogs and tacos. so
   W
   we decided to eat tacos.

4. When we finished eating, we went back to the field. but we saw other
                                                     W
   kids were playing, and we waited and waited. but they didn't leave, so
                                               T
   finally we decided to go home and watch some TV.

5. My friends and I wanted to watch some TV, so we bought some soda and popped some popcorn. Then we sat down, eager to see our favorite programs.

6. Just then my brother and a couple of his friends ran into the room. They were yelling about the big game being on that night. They just changed the channels and pushed us out of the way.

7. I told Mom what had just happened and how we had been there first. I told her about all the plans we had made. It wasn't fair that my brother should take over the TV without even asking us if it was okay.

8. My brother said I could watch my shows anytime, but the game was for the championship. He had asked for the TV earlier in the day, so he had a right to watch it.

9. Mom got angry because we were yelling at each other and not listening to her, so She turned off the TV and told our friends to go home. Then we had to sit down and do our homework.

10. My friends and I were having a good time, and my brother ruined it by taking over the TV. His friends didn't help matters either, and Mom finally got angry. It just wasn't fair!

Next Step: Write a paragraph about a recent exciting experience. First, write it with rambling sentences. Then go back and correct the mistakes.

Subject-Verb Agreement 1

The subject and the verb in a sentence must "agree" in number. This means that if the subject is singular, the verb must be singular. If the subject is plural, the verb must be plural. In the example sentences below, the subject is underlined once, and the verb is underlined twice.

Junior runs every night after school.

(The subject "Junior" and the verb "runs" agree because they are both singular.)

His friends usually play basketball.

(The subject "friends" and the verb "play" agree because they are both plural.)

Directions ▶ Read the sentences below. Subjects are underlined once, and verbs are underlined twice. If the verb agrees with its subject, write "C" on the line. If the verb does not agree with its subject, cross out the verb and write the correct verb above it. The first one has been done for you.

_____ 1. My school ~~have~~ *has* a band.

__C__ 2. In my class, most people play an instrument.

_____ 3. Flutes ~~is~~ *are* the most popular instrument this year.

_____ 4. Mr. Williams ~~are~~ *is* the band teacher.

_____ 5. He ~~make~~ *makes* us want to work hard for the band.

__C__ 6. Sometimes he is very funny.

_____ 7. We ~~plays~~ *play* marches and some popular songs, too.

_____ 8. In ninth grade, we ~~gets~~ *get* real band uniforms.

_____ 9. My friend Tamika ~~play~~ *plays* the piccolo.

__C__ 10. The piccolo is a small flute.

Next Step: Write three sentences about a musical instrument that you play or might like to play. Share your work with a classmate. Make sure that your verbs agree with your subjects.

Subject-Verb Agreement 2

A compound subject can make subject-verb agreement challenging. Remember that two or more simple subjects make a compound subject: *Lisa* and *Antonio* is the compound subject in the example below.

Lisa and Antonio like each other.

(Use the plural verb "like" because the compound subject is connected by "and.")

Either my sisters or Kevin always cracks a joke.

(Use the singular verb "cracks" because the compound subjects are connected by "or," and the verb agrees with the singular subject closer to it—"Kevin.")

> **Directions** If the subject and verb agree in the following sentences, write "C" on the line. If the subject and verb do not agree, correct the verb. The first one has been done for you.

_____ 1. Mike, Ynez, and Anna ~~eats~~ *eat* healthful foods.

_____ 2. Fruits and vegetables ~~is~~ *are* among their favorite foods.

__C__ 3. Grain and dairy products form a large part of their diets.

_____ 4. Either a sandwich or yogurt ~~are~~ *is* usually in Mike's lunch bag.

__C__ 5. Lettuce, tomato, and cheese make a good sandwich for Mike's lunch.

_____ 6. Mike, Ynez, and Anna always ~~brings~~ *bring* fruit.

__C__ 7. An apple, a pear, or a banana is a healthful dessert.

_____ 8. An orange or grapes ~~is~~ *are* good, too.

_____ 9. Mike and Ynez usually ~~packs~~ *pack* their own lunches.

_____ 10. Raw carrots and broccoli ~~is~~ *are* often included.

__C__ 11. Ynez's brother and sisters watch their diets, too.

Next Step: Write three sentences about a food you like to eat. Tell how healthful this food is. Use compound subjects, and make sure that your verbs agree with the subjects. Share your work with a classmate.

Subject-Verb Agreement 3

When a sentence has a compound subject, the subject and verb must agree in number. Use a plural verb if the compound subject uses *and* as a connector. If the compound subject uses *or* or *nor* as a connector, the verb must agree with the subject closest to the verb. In the following sentences, each subject is underlined once, and each verb is underlined twice.

Ramon and Teresa speak Spanish.
(Use the plural verb "speak" because the compound subject is connected by "and.")

Neither the boys nor Teresa speaks French.
(Use the singular verb "speaks" because the compound subject is connected by "nor," and the singular subject "Teresa" is closest to the verb.)

Directions ▶ Read the sentences. Subjects are underlined once, and verbs are underlined twice. If the verb agrees with the subject, write "C" on the line. If the verb does not agree, cross it out and write the correct verb above it. The first one has been done for you.

_____ 1. To some people, Spanish and Italian ~~sounds~~ *sound* similar.

__C__ 2. Mexico and Spain are Spanish-speaking countries.

_____ 3. Teresa and Jake ~~wants~~ *want* to study French next year.

__C__ 4. Neither Ramon nor Gabrielle studies French now.

_____ 5. Ramon and Teresa ~~uses~~ *use* Spanish at home.

_____ 6. Their older brother and sister ~~knows~~ *know* the language well.

__C__ 7. Ramon's mother and father come from Nicaragua.

_____ 8. Either David or Jeff ~~help~~ *helps* their German teacher grade papers.

_____ 9. Takahiro and his brother ~~reads~~ *reads* Japanese.

_C_ **10.** Japanese <u>magazines</u> and <u>newspapers</u> <u><u>arrive</u></u> at their house weekly.

_____ **11.** Takahiro's <u>parents</u> and <u>grandparents</u> ~~<u><u>wants</u></u>~~ *want* him to learn more of the

language.

_____ **12.** Neither Takahiro's <u>brother</u> nor his <u>cousins</u> ~~<u><u>writes</u></u>~~ *write* Japanese well.

Directions ➤ Use each compound subject below in your own sentence. Make sure that the verbs agree with the subjects.

1. Cats and kittens

Cats and kittens are fun house pets.

_____

2. Neither snow nor ice

Neither snow nor ice stops the mail.

_____

3. Elizabeth or her sisters

Elizabeth or her sisters have to finish the dishes.

_____

4. Men or women

Men or women are welcome to apply for the job.

_____

5. Three girls and a boy

Three girls and a boy were on the bus.

_____

Next Step: Choose a final draft from your writing portfolio (or a selection your teacher gives you). Underline all the subjects once and all the verbs twice in your sentences. Make sure that all of the subjects and verbs agree.

Subject-Verb Agreement 4

An indefinite pronoun can be a subject. If the indefinite pronoun is singular, the verb is singular. If it is plural, the verb is plural. Sometimes the indefinite pronoun can be either singular or plural, depending on its meaning in a sentence.

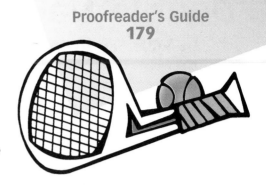

SINGULAR INDEFINITE PRONOUNS					
each	one	everything	something	anyone	nothing
either	everyone	someone	anybody	nobody	another
neither	everybody	somebody	anything	no one	

PLURAL INDEFINITE PRONOUNS		SINGULAR OR PLURAL INDEFINITE PRONOUNS				
both	many	all	any	most	none	some

Many enjoy watching people play tennis.

("Many" is plural, so the verb "enjoy" is plural.)

Everyone likes a close match.

("Everyone" is singular, so the verb "likes" is singular.)

Most of the fans understand how to keep score.

(The verb "understand" is plural because "most" refers" to "fans," which is plural.)

Most of the game consists of serving and volleying.

(The verb "consists" is singular because "most" refers to "game," which is singular.)

> **Directions** ▶ The subjects are underlined once and the verbs twice. Write "C" if the subject and verb agree. If they do not agree, correct the verb. The first two have been done for you.

_C_ **1.** Alandra and Selina enjoy tennis.

_____ **2.** Either ~~are~~ *is* a good player.

_____ **3.** Both ~~wants~~ *want* to start playing right away.

_____ **4.** Either ~~keep~~ *keeps* score during the game.

_____ **5.** Each of them ~~play~~ *plays* after school at the high school.

_C_ **6.** Neither likes to warm up.

_____ **7.** Some of the school courts ~~needs~~ *need* resurfacing.

Double Negatives 1

A **double negative** occurs when you use two negative words (*never* and *no*; *no* and *not*) together in a sentence. Words like *hardly, barely,* or *scarcely* are considered negatives.   There may be more than one way to correct a double negative.

Double Negative:	**They <u>won't</u> fight <u>no</u> one.**
Corrected:	**They won't fight anyone.**
Corrected:	**They will fight no one.**
Double Negative:	**They did <u>not</u> have <u>no</u> popcorn.**
Corrected:	**They did not have any popcorn.**
Double Negative:	**I <u>can't</u> <u>hardly</u> run today.**
Corrected:	**I can hardly run today.**

Directions ▶ Correct the double negatives in the following sentences. The first sentence has been done for you.

Answers will vary.

1. Ali went to the store, but he didn't buy ~~nothing~~. *anything*

2. Nolan tried several times to start his car, but he didn't have ~~no~~ luck. *any*

3. Lateesha won't ~~never~~ eat hamburgers again. *ever*

4. Although the rain fell all day, the river did not rise ~~no~~ higher. *any*

5. Runyan ~~couldn't~~ find no gym shoes for the game. *could*

6. Yesterday was so foggy Kevin couldn't see ~~nothing~~. *anything*

7. Lucinda ~~couldn't~~ barely watch the monster movie. *could*

8. Joey said he didn't know ~~nothing~~ about the broken window. *anything*

9. Maurice ~~can't~~ hardly move because of his sunburn. *can*

10. Tyson said he ~~did not need~~ no help with his math problems. *needed*

11. Fran said she ~~never~~ knew nothing about ~~no~~ animals escaping from the zoo.

12. Tress said she didn't like that singer ~~no~~ more. *any*

Double Negatives 2

Here's more practice to help you avoid double negatives in your writing.

Double Negative: **I don't want none.**
Corrected: **I don't want any.**

> **Directions** ➤ Correct any sentences that contain double negatives. There are 11 double negatives besides the corrected one.

Answers will vary.

1   Last summer Will invited his friend Sam to visit him in Montana for

                                        any

2   a trip to Glacier Park. Sam didn't have ~~no~~ money, so he didn't ~~hardly~~ know

3   how he would get to such a faraway place. His mom told him that she and

4   his dad would pay for the trip. As Sam packed, he tried not to forget

     anything

5   ~~nothing.~~ After a long bus ride, he finally got to Will's town, Great Falls.

6   The next day on the way to Glacier Park, they saw antelope, deer, and

                          any

7   prairie dogs, but they didn't see ~~no~~ wolves. Glacier Park is a beautiful place,

                                                           ever

8   but it was a little frightening for Sam, who lived in a city. He hadn't ~~never~~

9   been in the wilderness. He wanted to hike, but he was worried. He didn't

          any

10   want to run into ~~no~~ bears. Because Sam was scared, Will ~~never~~ told him

11   nothing about the bear tracks near their cabin.

                                              saw

12   In the morning they climbed a mountain. They ~~didn't see~~ nobody else

13   on the trail. Then it got harder and harder for Sam to breathe. He realized

     could   *any*

14   he ~~couldn't~~ barely walk. He thought he wouldn't be able to go ~~no~~ farther.

15   Sam didn't know that the air gets thinner at higher elevations. Suddenly he

                  could

16   felt dizzy, and he ~~couldn't~~ hardly see a thing. Will told Sam to sit down and

17   rest. After a while, Sam felt better, and they hiked to the summit. Sam was

18   pleased as he looked around and saw the mountain peaks in the distance.

                                anything

19   He knew he would never forget ~~nothing~~ about this trip.

Double Subjects

A **double subject** occurs when a pronoun is used immediately after the subject. Sentences with double subjects are a common problem.

Double Subject: **Carmen she slipped on the ice.**
Corrected: **Carmen slipped on the ice.**

Directions ▶ Read the following story. Circle the unnecessary pronouns that make double subjects. The first one has been done for you. There are nine double subjects besides the corrected one.

1 Last week Samantha and some friends decided to go to a movie. Sue

2 and Lanesha (they) wanted to see something scary. Samantha really doesn't

3 like to be scared, but she went with them anyway. In the movie a huge,

4 ugly hand (it) reached out of the shadows to grab one of the actors. Everyone

5 in the theater screamed. Samantha (she) knew this was not real, but she was

6 frightened anyway. Sue and Lanesha (they) were just as scared.

7 At last the movie was over, and it was time to go home. The girls (they)

8 forgot it would be dark. They began walking home. They bravely laughed

9 and joked, but every unlit alley bothered them. Suddenly, they stopped.

10 They saw something in the shadows. That something (it) moved. Sue and

11 Lanesha screamed and ran. Samantha just stood there. Then Samantha

12 (she) heard some noise behind her, and she took off running, too. After they

13 got to Samantha's house, they hid behind the kitchen door. Then they heard

14 Samantha's brother laughing. Her brother (he) had been at the movie, too.

15 He had decided to play a trick on the girls. The girls (they) were mad, so

16 they chased him out of the house. Samantha, Sue, and Lanesha (they) agreed

17 never to go to another monster movie at night.

Sentence Combining: Key Words

You can combine short sentences by moving a key word from one sentence to another. Often the key word is an adjective or adverb.

Short Sentences: **Mia rode her new bike. She rode it <u>carefully</u>.**

Combined with Adverb: **Mia rode her new bike carefully.**

Short Sentences: **It was a gorgeous sunset. It was <u>orange</u>.**

Combined with Adjective: **It was a gorgeous orange sunset.**

> **Directions** Use an adjective or adverb to combine each pair of sentences. The first sentence has been done for you.

1. Vegetable soup is my favorite. I like it spicy. (*adjective*)

Spicy vegetable soup is my favorite.

2. Jamal goes to the movies. He goes to the movies often. (*adverb*)

Jamal often goes to the movies.

3. We won tickets to a football game. There were five tickets. (*adjective*)

We won five tickets to a football game.

4. Paul and Haley are running. They are running quickly. (*adverb*)

Paul and Haley are running quickly.

5. Damian helped his mother clean. He helped her gladly. (*adverb*)

Damian gladly helped his mother clean.

6. I like your haircut. Your haircut is short. (*adjective*)

I like your short haircut.

7. The canary sings softly. The canary is yellow. (*adjective*)

The yellow canary sings softly.

Next Step: Write freely for 5 minutes about a movie or sporting event. Find sets of short sentences that could be combined using a key word (an adjective or adverb).

Sentence Combining: Key Words and Phrases

Proofreader's Guide
151, 154, 175, 186

Use key words and phrases to combine ideas
from shorter sentences.

Short Sentences:	**Todd has guitar lessons.** **The lessons are <u>on Monday nights</u>.**
Combined with Prepositional Phrase:	**Todd has guitar lessons on Monday nights.**
Short Sentences:	**Grandpa will visit us. He will visit us <u>soon</u>.**
Combined with Key Word:	**Grandpa will visit us soon.**
Short Sentences:	**This spring was <u>short</u>. It was <u>cold</u>. It was <u>wet</u>.**
Combined with Series of Words:	**This spring was short, cold, and wet.**
Short Sentences:	**At practice we learn <u>plays</u>. We <u>scrimmage</u>.**
Combined with Compound Verb:	**At practice we learn plays and scrimmage.**
Short Sentences:	**<u>Chris</u> sleeps late. <u>Cody</u> sleeps late.**
Combined with Compound Subject:	**Chris and Cody sleep late.**

Directions ▷ Combine each group of short sentences into one longer sentence. The words in parentheses tell you which method to use. The first one has been done for you.

1. The new chairs are big. They are soft. They are comfortable. (*series of words*)

The new chairs are big, soft, and comfortable.

2. Preston dried the dishes. He put away the dishes. (*compound verb*)

Preston dried and put away the dishes.

3. Maurice found the key. The key was under the sofa. (*prepositional phrase*)

Maurice found the key under the sofa.

4. The elevator in my building got stuck. It happened yesterday. (*key word*)

The elevator in my building got stuck yesterday.

5. Albert likes loud fireworks. I like loud fireworks, too. (*compound subject*)

Albert and I like loud fireworks.

Sentence Combining: Coordinating Conjunctions 1

Proofreader's Guide
152, 186

A simple sentence has one independent clause. It states one complete thought. A compound sentence has two or more independent clauses (or simple sentences), a comma, and a coordinating conjunction such as *and, or, for, but, so,* and *yet.*

Simple Sentences: **August is hot. We swim a lot during that month.**

Combined: **August is hot, so we swim a lot during that month.**

(The coordinating conjunction "so" connects these sentences.)

Directions ▶ Combine each pair of short sentences into one longer sentence using a coordinating conjunction. The first one has been done for you. *Answers will vary.*

1. Lions and tigers are similar. They are different in some ways.

Lions and tigers are similar, but they are different in some ways.

2. Lions live in groups called prides. Tigers live alone.

Lions live in groups called prides, but tigers live alone.

3. Jaguars and leopards look a lot alike. Jaguars are larger.

Jaguars and leopards look a lot alike, yet jaguars are larger.

4. Jaguars live in Central and South America. Leopards roam southern Asia and Africa.

Jaguars live in Central and South America, and leopards roam southern

Asia and Africa.

5. Panthers are black leopards with spots. Their spots are hard to see.

Panthers are black leopards with spots, but their spots are hard to

see.

6. Most cats do not like the water. Tigers are good swimmers.

Most cats do not like the water, yet tigers are good swimmers.

1. Lois Lowry is an author of books for children. She has won major awards for her books.

   Lois Lowry is an author of books for children, and she has won major awards for her books.

2. Lois Lowry was born in Hawaii. Later she lived in Japan on an army base.

   Lois Lowry was born in Hawaii, but later she lived in Japan on an army base.

3. This experience was important. It gave her ideas for the plots of some of her stories.

   This experience was important, for it gave her ideas for the plots of some of her stories.

4. She wrote the "Anastasia Krupnik" books. She is also the author of *Number the Stars* and *The Giver*.

   She wrote the "Anastasia Krupnik" books, and she is also the author of Number the Stars and The Giver.

5. Lowry often writes about humorous family events. She also tackles serious issues.

   Lowry often writes about humorous family events, but she also tackles serious issues.

6. Some of her characters make hard decisions. Some act very bravely.

   Some of her characters make hard decisions, and some act very bravely.

Sentence Combining: Coordinating Conjunctions 2

Proofreader's Guide
152, 186

A simple sentence includes only one independent clause. A compound sentence is made up of two or more simple sentences, usually joined by a comma and a coordinating conjunction—*and, or, but, nor,* or *so.*

Simple Sentences: **I got a new mouse pad. This one is very colorful.**

Combined: **I got a new mouse pad, and this one is very colorful.**

(The coordinating conjunction "and" connects these sentences.)

> **Directions** ⟩ Combine each pair of sentences below into one compound sentence, using a comma and a coordinating conjunction. The first one has been done for you. *Answers will vary.*

1. I need a new computer. I need to add memory to my old one.

I need a new computer, or I need to add memory to my old one.

2. The one I have still works. It is very slow.

The one I have still works, but it is very slow.

3. Tyree knows which system to get. It is on sale now.

Tyree knows which system to get, and it is on sale now.

4. Dad does not want to spend too much. That low price should please him.

Dad does not want to spend too much, so that low price should please him.

5. Mom thinks I'll only play games. I'll use the computer for homework, too.

Mom thinks I'll only play games, but I'll use the computer for homework, too.

Next Step: Choose two of your compound sentences above and join them with a different coordinating conjunction.

Sentence Combining: Subordinating Conjunctions 1

Proofreader's Guide
152, 176, 186

You can combine two simple sentences into one complex sentence. One way to do this is to use a subordinating conjunction. Words such as *after, when, since, because, though,* and *before* are subordinating conjunctions. *Note:* Do not use a comma when the dependent clause is at the end of the sentence.

Simple Sentences: **Roy is wearing his best suit.**
He is attending his sister's wedding.

Combined with "Because": **Roy is wearing his best suit because he is attending his sister's wedding.**
("Because" introduces the dependent clause.)

Directions ▶ Combine the following short sentences into complex sentences. Use the words given in parentheses to connect the sentences. The first one has been done for you.

1. Winter days are short in Sweden. It is located far to the north. (*because*)

   Winter days are short in Sweden because it is located far to the north.

2. The phone rang 10 times. Ilana was writing her report. (*while*)

   The phone rang 10 times while Ilana was writing her report.

3. The alarm went off. Lorene had left for school. (*after*)

   The alarm went off after Lorene had left for school.

4. Rayna takes the subway. The buses aren't running. (*if*)

   Rayna takes the subway if the buses aren't running.

5. Chen did warm-ups. He ran around the track five times. (*before*)

   Chen did warm-ups before he ran around the track five times.

Next Step: Write two short sentences that can be combined into a complex sentence. Exchange with a classmate and combine each other's sentences using a subordinating conjunction.

Sentence Combining: Subordinating Conjunctions 2

Proofreader's Guide
152, 176, 186

Subordinating conjunctions such as *after, until, when, since, because,* or *before* can be used to combine sentences. Two sentences combined with a subordinating conjunction become a complex sentence. *Note:* Do not use a comma when the dependent clause is at the end of the sentence.

Simple Sentences:	**My cat lost his hearing. He was 12 years old.**
Combined:	**My cat lost his hearing when he was 12 years old.**
	("When" introduces the dependent clause at the end of the new complex sentence.)

Simple Sentences:	**My dog got sick. I took him to the vet.**
Combined:	**When my dog got sick, I took him to the vet.**
	("When" introduces the dependent clause at the beginning of the new complex sentence and a comma separates the clause from the rest of the sentence.)

Directions ❯ Use the directions in parentheses to combine each pair of sentences. The first one has been done for you.

1. Animal care is hard work. Animals can have health problems.
   (*Use "because" with the dependent clause at the end of the sentence.*)

   Animal care is hard work because animals can have health problems.

2. Animals have surgery. They shouldn't touch their stitches.
   (*Use "after" with the dependent clause at the beginning of the sentence.*)

   After animals have surgery, they shouldn't touch their stitches.

3. It was difficult to stop animals from disturbing their stitches. Someone designed a device.
   (*Use "until" with the dependent clause at the end of the sentence.*)

   It was difficult to stop animals from disturbing their stitches until

   someone designed a device .

4. The lampshade-shaped collar looks funny. It keeps animals from taking out their stitches.
(*Use "although" with the dependent clause at the beginning of the sentence.*)

Although the lampshade-shaped collar looks funny, it keeps animals

from taking out their stitches.

5. The protective collar is removed after the surgery has healed. The animal's recovery continues to be a concern.
(*Use "although" with the dependent clause at the beginning of the sentence.*)

Although the protective collar is removed after the surgery has

healed, the animal's recovery continues to be a concern.

6. Reed bought two snakes as pets. He read about the different kinds.
(*Use "before" with the dependent clause at the end of the sentence.*)

Reed bought two snakes as pets before he read about the different

kinds.

7. Avery played with his new dog. He was pleased by his pet's affection.
(*Use "when" with the dependent clause at the beginning of the sentence.*)

When Avery played with his new dog, he was pleased by his pet's

affection.

8. Pets provide happiness and comfort to people of all ages. It is not surprising that they are popular companions.
(*Use "since" with the dependent clause at the beginning of the sentence.*)

Since pets provide happiness and comfort to people of all ages, it is

not surprising that they are popular companions.

9. Alex races with his dog. His younger sister Berrie cuddles with their kitten.
(*Use "whereas" with the dependent clause at the end of the sentence.*)

Alex races with his dog whereas his younger sister Berrie cuddles with

their kitten.

Next Step: Write three complex sentences about a pet or another animal. Exchange your work with a classmate. Underline the three subordinating conjunctions that your partner used.

Sentence Combining: Relative Pronouns 1

You can use relative pronouns—words such as *who, whose, or which*—to combine two simple sentences into one complex sentence.

Simple Sentences: **The flag waved in the breeze.**
The flag was raised outside the school.

Combined: **The flag, which was raised outside the school, waved in the breeze.** (Combining the two sentences with the word "which" creates a longer, clearer sentence.)

 **Directions** Combine each of the following pairs of sentences to make a complex sentence. Use the relative pronoun in parentheses. The first one has been done for you.

1. The river overflowed its banks.
The river flooded the city and the surrounding area. (*which*)

The river, which overflowed its banks, flooded the city and the

surrounding area.

2. Sandbags prevented much damage.
Sandbags had been prepared weeks in advance. (*which*)

Sandbags, which had been prepared weeks in advance, prevented much

damage.

3. Volunteers stacked the sandbags.
Volunteers came from all parts of the city. (*who*)

Volunteers, who came from all parts of the city, stacked the sandbags.

4. Many people on Main Street cheered when the flood receded.
The houses of many people on Main Street had water in them. (*whose*)

Many people on Main Street, whose houses had water in them, cheered

when the flood receded.

Next Step: Write a pair of sentences that could be combined using "which" or "who." Exchange them with a classmate.

Sentence Combining: Relative Pronouns 2

Relative pronouns—words such as *who, whose,* and *which*—are used to combine two simple sentences into one complex sentence.

Simple Sentences: **Ellie writes her own comic strip. She draws funny hippos.**

Combined: **Ellie, who draws funny hippos, writes her own comic strip.**
(Combining the two sentences with the word "who" creates a longer, clearer sentence.)

Directions ➤ Combine the following pairs of sentences to form complex sentences. Use the relative pronouns in parentheses. The first one has been done for you.

1. The cartoonist Matt Groening created <u>The Simpsons</u>. He was born in 1954. (*who*)

The cartoonist Matt Groening, who was born in 1954, created The

Simpsons.

2. Bart Simpson is one main character. He always gets into trouble. (*who*)

Bart Simpson, who always gets into trouble, is one main character.

3. The cartoon "Dilbert" is about working in an office. The cartoon was created by Scott Adams. (*which*)

The cartoon "Dilbert," which was created by Scott Adams, is about

working in an office.

4. Hank Ketcham was a popular illustrator. His comic strip was called "Dennis the Menace." (*whose*)

Hank Ketcham, whose comic strip was called "Dennis the Menace," was

a popular illustrator.

Next Step: Write three complex sentences about something you have read or seen on TV. Include a different relative pronoun in each sentence. Share your work with a partner.

Parts of Speech Activities

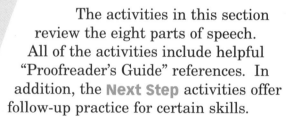

The activities in this section review the eight parts of speech. All of the activities include helpful "Proofreader's Guide" references. In addition, the **Next Step** activities offer follow-up practice for certain skills.

Using Nouns

Nouns name people, places, things, and ideas.

Titanic **was a** movie **that was full of** suspense.
("*Titanic*" names a movie, "movie" names a thing, and "suspense" names an idea.)

The film **filled the** theater **with** moviegoers.
("Film" names a thing, "theater" names a place, and "moviegoers" names people.)

> **Directions** ▶ Underline the nouns in each of the following sentences. The number at the end of each sentence tells you how many nouns you should find. The first one has been done for you.

1. The movie was based on the tragic story of a famous ship. *(3)*

2. Our class became interested in the tragedy after seeing the film. *(3)*

3. Many books have also been written about the ship. *(2)*

4. The *Titanic* was advertised as the safest ship of its time. *(3)*

5. The ship sailed out of Queenstown, Ireland and into the North Atlantic on April 11, 1912. *(6)*

6. The North Atlantic was a dangerous place with many icebergs. *(3)*

7. The ship hit an iceberg and began to sink. *(2)*

8. Many people drowned, despite a rescue attempt. *(2)*

9. Some of the passengers showed great bravery. *(2)*

10. Families felt great sorrow after the ship sank and lives were lost. *(4)*

11. In 1985, a research team found the *Titanic* on the bottom of the ocean. *(5)*

12. The ship was in two pieces 13,000 feet below the surface. *(4)*

13. In 1996, special tests showed that only a small portion (13 square feet) of the hull was damaged by the iceberg. *(6)*

Categorize the following 24 nouns according to the headings below. Four have been categorized for you.

joy	Sabrina	telescope	pens	school
China	eyes	beauty	mechanic	freedom
truck	New York	sofa	confusion	Greg
college	Lucille	sister	monkey	park
Dr. Sanjeev	anger	library	peace	

■ People

Sabrina

Lucille

Dr. Sanjeev

sister

Greg

mechanic

■ Places

college

school

New York

China

library

park

■ Things

telescope

monkey

pens

truck

eyes

sofa

■ Ideas

anger

peace

confusion

joy

freedom

beauty

Next Step: Write three sentences about what you see on your way to school. Underline the nouns in your sentences, and label each one as either "person," "place," "thing," or "idea." Share your work with a classmate.

Singular and Plural Nouns

Singular nouns name one person, place, thing, or idea. **Plural nouns** name more than one person, place, thing, or idea.

The baby slept in the crib for a short time.
(The three nouns in this sentence are singular. Each one refers to one person, thing, or idea.)

My older sisters never sleep for more than five hours on school nights.
(The three nouns in this sentence are plural. Each one refers to more than one person, thing, or idea.)

Directions > In the sentences that follow, underline each noun. Write "S" over each singular noun and "P" over each plural noun. The number of nouns in each sentence is in parentheses. The first sentence has been done for you.

1. There are seven continents on our planet, all of different sizes. *(3)*
   P   S   P

2. Geography is a subject of great interest to many people. *(4)*
   S   S   S   P

3. In class, Ms. Han gave us facts about different places. *(4)*
   S   S   P   P

4. Central America is a strip of land between Mexico and Colombia. *(5)*
   S   S   S   S   S

5. Portuguese, not Spanish, is the official language of Brazil, the largest country
   S   S   S   S   S
   in South America. *(6)*
      S

6. Africa is surrounded almost entirely by water. *(2)*
   S   S

7. Australia is really an island. *(2)*
   S   S

8. Antarctica has few people and few settlements. *(3)*
   S   P   P

9. Visitors there may find beauty in its ice and snow. *(4)*
   P   S   S   S

10. Sometimes Europe and Asia together are called Eurasia. *(3)*
            S   S   S

11. Even though they are joined by land, each is a separate continent. *(2)*
                            S   S

Common and Proper Nouns

A **common noun** is any noun that does not name a specific person, place, thing, or idea.

woman   park   planet   language

A **proper noun** does name a specific person, place, thing, or idea. Proper nouns are capitalized.

Lila   Davis Park   Saturn   Spanish

Directions Underline the nouns in the following sentences. The number of nouns is in parentheses. Write "C" above each common noun and "P" above each proper noun. The first sentence has been done for you.

           C   P   C   P

1. The <u>book</u> *Gulliver's Travels* was written by <u>author</u> <u>Jonathan Swift</u>. *(4)*

    P

2. <u>Swift</u> was born in the seventeenth <u>century</u> in <u>Dublin</u>, <u>Ireland</u>. *(4)*

3. Although his <u>parents</u> had little <u>money</u>, wealthy <u>relatives</u> paid for him to go to <u>school</u> and travel to <u>England</u>. *(5)*

4. <u>Swift</u> was critical of the <u>behavior</u> of many of the <u>people</u> he met. *(3)*

5. He thought that his <u>books</u> might influence <u>people</u> to behave differently. *(2)*

6. He used unusual <u>titles</u> like *A Tale of a Tub*, and <u>readers</u> liked that. *(3)*

7. He published *Gulliver's Travels*, which made <u>fun</u> of <u>books</u> about <u>travel</u>. *(4)*

8. This <u>book</u> shows <u>people</u> and <u>animals</u> behaving in silly <u>ways</u>. *(4)*

9. <u>Swift</u> suffered from a <u>disease</u> that caused <u>dizziness</u>. *(3)*

10. When he died, he left his <u>money</u> to build a <u>hospital</u> in <u>Dublin</u>. *(3)*

Next Step: Write three sentences about a trip you have taken to another neighborhood or another city. Describe what you saw there. Then underline all of the nouns; label them "C" for common noun and "P" for proper noun. Exchange papers with a classmate and check each other's work.

Count and Noncount Nouns 1

Count nouns are words that can be counted. They can have *a, an,* or *one* in front of them, and they can be singular or plural. **Noncount nouns** cannot be counted or have *a, an,* or *one* in front of them. Noncount nouns do not have a plural form..

- ■ Count   a shoe   an example
- ■ Noncount   sugar   furniture

Directions Circle all noncount nouns in the following sentences. The first one has been done for you.

1. The (luggage) cost a lot of (money).

2. The (thunder) followed the (lightning).

3. His (honesty) is admirable.

4. Joe's sister saw piles of (snow).

5. He drinks (milk) and (juice).

6. I have to buy a jar of (mustard).

Directions In each of the following sentences, one noun is underlined. If it is a count noun, write "C" on the blank. If it is a noncount noun, write "N" on the blank. The first two have been done for you.

_N_ 1. Bees produce <u>honey</u> from flowers.

_C_ 2. When I saw the bread, I knew I wanted a <u>piece</u>.

_N_ 3. Emmanuel is no longer afraid of the <u>dark</u>.

_N_ 4. Sweden produces fine <u>furniture</u>.

_N_ 5. It wasn't much <u>fun</u> clearing all the weeds.

_C_ 6. The barn was too small for three <u>horses</u>.

_C_ 7. I like turkey <u>sandwiches</u>.

_C_ 8. Flowers were growing in the vacant <u>lot</u>.

_N_ 9. You never know what type of <u>weather</u> to expect.

Count and Noncount Nouns 2

Practice identifying and using count and noncount nouns in the exercise below.

- ■ **Count**   **strength**   **potato**
- ■ **Noncount**   **music**   **rice**

Directions ⟩ Each of the following sentences has one count noun and one noncount noun. Underline each count noun and circle each noncount noun. The first sentence has been done for you.

1. The (luggage) could not hold all of her shoes.

2. Three boys played in the (snow).

3. The (fur) of a cat may be short or long.

4. (Sleet) fell over the city.

5. The boy loved to eat (sugar).

6. High (humidity) can make a person tired.

7. A man ran quickly to escape the (rain).

8. All students did their (homework).

9. (Perspiration) dripped from her forehead.

10. My next class is (music).

11. (Thunder) can frighten a dog.

12. (Salt) is harvested from the Great Salt Lake.

13. Visible (light) is made up of many colors.

14. (Honesty) is the best policy.

15. His sandwich had too much (pepper).

Next Step: Choose five noncount nouns and use them in sentences.

Uses of Nouns 1

Proofreader's Guide
158, 159, 177

Nouns are used in different ways in different sentences. Three uses are shown below.

■ **Subject Noun**

The <u>teacher</u> is in the lunchroom.
(The subject noun "teacher" is the part of the sentence that is doing something or being discussed.)

■ **Predicate Noun**

Mr. Lucas is my favorite <u>teacher</u>.
(The predicate noun "teacher" follows the linking verb "is" and renames the subject "Mr. Lucas.")

■ **Possessive Noun**

The <u>teacher's</u> grade book was left in the cafeteria.
(The possessive noun "teacher's" shows ownership.)

Directions ▶ Label each of the underlined nouns below. Write "SN" for subject noun, "PN" for predicate noun, or "POS" for possessive noun. The first sentence has been done for you.

POS **1.** <u>Juanita's</u> house is for sale.

_PN_ **2.** It was the <u>property</u> of her grandparents.

_SN_ **3.** <u>Juanita</u> is moving to Minnesota.

_SN_ **4.** <u>Tonisha</u> came to visit her last week.

_PN_ **5.** They are best <u>friends</u>.

POS **6.** <u>Tonisha's</u> family will miss her.

_PN_ **7.** Roberto is Juanita's <u>cousin</u>.

POS **8.** <u>Roberto's</u> family will visit for a week in the summer.

_SN_ **9.** <u>Summer</u> is a good time to visit Minnesota.

_SN_ **10.** The <u>family</u> plans to go fishing and biking.

Label the underlined nouns in the sentences below. Write "SN" for subject noun, "PN" for predicate noun, or "POS" for possessive noun. The first sentence has been done for you.

      SN   *POS*   *PN*

1. The <u>wind</u> was the <u>storm's</u> biggest <u>danger</u>.

     POS   *SN*

2. The <u>house's</u> <u>roof</u> was damaged in the storm.

     POS

3. <u>Candy's</u> parents were at work at the time.

       SN

4. Her <u>relatives</u> urged her to stay with them.

      SN   *PN*

5. Her <u>aunt</u> is her best <u>friend</u>.

            POS

6. Her uncle took <u>Marisol's</u> car to get Candy.

         SN   *PN*

7. The howling <u>noise</u> was the <u>sound</u> of the wind.

       SN   *PN*

8. The <u>storm</u> was a gully <u>washer</u> in their area.

        SN

9. Their <u>electricity</u> was out for a while.

                                       PN

10. In Candy's part of the city, this was the worst <u>storm</u> in many years.

       POS

11. Many <u>people's</u> properties were damaged.

   SN   *POS*

12. <u>Trees</u> fell, and many of the <u>city's</u> power lines were down for days.

      SN   *PN*

13. The fallen <u>trees</u> were <u>trouble</u> for the city's residents.

      SN   *PN*

14. Volunteer <u>workers</u> were a <u>blessing</u>.

      POS

15. The power <u>company's</u> crews worked overtime to restore electricity to all

residences.

Next Step: Write three or four sentences about a storm that you experienced. Label the subject nouns (SN), predicate nouns (PN), and possessive nouns (POS) in your sentences.

Uses of Nouns 2

Sometimes nouns are used as objects. Here are three types of object nouns:

■ A **direct object** answers the question *what?* or *whom?* after an action verb.

Mrs. Wade took a trip.
(The direct object "trip" answers the question "Mrs. Wade took *what*?")

■ An **indirect object** names the person or thing *to whom* or *for whom* something is done. It comes after an action verb, but before the direct object.

Mrs. Wade gave her travel agent a check.
(The indirect object "travel agent" names the person "to whom" the check was given. "Mrs. Wade gave a check *to whom*?")

■ An **object of a preposition** is the noun or pronoun at the end of a prepositional phrase.

Mrs. Wade took a trip to Chicago.
("To Chicago" is a prepositional phrase; "Chicago" is the object of the preposition "to.")

> **Directions**

In the following sentences, label the underlined nouns. Write "IO" for indirect objects, "DO" for direct objects, and "OP" for objects of a preposition. The first sentence has been done for you.

OP **1.** Ariana decided to take the subway to her grandmother's <u>house</u>.

DO **2.** Ariana did her <u>homework</u> before she left.

IO **3.** Mrs. Ramos gave <u>Ariana</u> a book to read on the train.

DO **4.** Ariana found a <u>seat</u> in the back.

OP **5.** She put her backpack on her <u>lap</u> and read the book.

DO **6.** She really liked the <u>book</u>.

IO **7.** She lent her <u>grandmother</u> the book.

Directions ➤ Label the underlined nouns in the following sentences. Write "DO" for direct objects, "IO" for indirect objects, and "OP" for objects of a preposition. The first sentence has been done for you.

                                         DO   *OP*

1. The rain pelted the <u>cornfield</u> across the <u>street</u>.

                              DO   *OP*

2. Juan and Carlos bought <u>flowers</u> for their <u>mother</u>.

                    OP   *OP*

3. Shells from the <u>ocean</u> washed up on the <u>shore</u>.

                        DO   *OP*

4. Kindergartners ate their <u>lunches</u> before <u>recess</u>.

                IO   *DO*

5. Hilda gave <u>Simone</u> the <u>paintbrushes</u>.

                       DO   *OP*

6. Many people bought their <u>tickets</u> for the <u>concert</u>.

                  OP

7. The seats in the <u>theater</u> were filled.

            DO   *OP*   *OP*

8. We found the <u>paint</u> for our <u>bicycles</u> at <u>Melville's Hardware Store</u>.

                          DO   *OP*

9. Dr. Jackson delivered an interesting <u>speech</u> to the <u>class</u>.

                IO   *DO*

10. Althea sent her <u>father</u> a <u>postcard</u>.

                   IO   *DO*

11. The Boy Scouts gave <u>Bob</u> its highest <u>award</u>.

              IO   *DO*

12. We showed the <u>cashier</u> our <u>receipt</u>.

              IO   *DO*

13. She offered <u>Grandma</u> a <u>mint</u>.

                DO   *OP*

14. Grandma asked <u>Norell</u> for another <u>mint</u>.

          OP   *DO*

15. After the <u>picnic</u>, Ben picked up the <u>plates</u> and pop cans.

                  IO   *DO*

16. The P.T.A. bought the <u>school</u> new playground <u>equipment</u>.

Next Step: Think of a picnic or class trip you have gone on. Describe it in three or four sentences. Label the object nouns in your sentences. Exchange sentences with a class-mate and check each other's labels.

Using Pronouns

Pronouns are words used in place of nouns. Without pronouns, we would keep repeating the same words.

■ **Without Pronouns**

<u>Don</u> asked <u>Don's</u> sister to help <u>Don</u>.

(This sentence uses the same word three times.)

■ **With Pronouns**

<u>Don</u> asked <u>his</u> sister to help <u>him</u>.

(The pronouns "his" and "him" make the sentence easier to read and say.)

SUBJECT		OBJECT		POSSESSIVE	
SINGULAR	PLURAL	SINGULAR	PLURAL	SINGULAR	PLURAL
I	we	me	us	my, mine	our, ours
you	you	you	you	your, yours	your, yours
he, she, it	they	him, her, it	them	his, her, hers, its	their, theirs

Directions ▶▶ Rewrite the following sentences, using a pronoun to replace each underlined noun.

1. Tessa asked <u>Tessa's</u> mother to drive <u>Tessa</u> to school.

Tessa asked her mother to drive her to school.

2. Tony was worried that <u>Tony</u> would forget to feed <u>Tony's</u> neighbor's fish.

Tony was worried that he would forget to feed his neighbor's fish.

3. Jenna and Anne wonder if <u>Jenna and Anne</u> can trust <u>Jenna and Anne's</u> brother to feed <u>Jenna and Anne's</u> cat Felix while <u>Jenna and Anne</u> are gone for a week.

Jenna and Anne wonder if they can trust their brother to feed their

cat Felix while they are gone for a week.

Underline the personal pronouns in each sentence. The number of pronouns is given in parentheses. The first sentence has been done for you.

1. <u>I</u> never knew much about ants until <u>my</u> brother wrote <u>his</u> report on <u>them</u>. *(4)*

2. Andy's report showed that <u>their</u> ways are sometimes similar to <u>our</u> ways. *(2)*

3. <u>They</u> live in colonies, and many of <u>them</u> are quite crowded. *(2)*

4. <u>You</u> could say <u>their</u> colonies are like <u>our</u> cities. *(3)*

5. <u>My</u> brother and <u>his</u> friend Stuart spent a lot of time on <u>their</u> report. *(3)*

6. <u>It</u> took <u>their</u> after-school time, and Stuart's mom was proud of <u>him</u>. *(3)*

7. <u>His</u> sister had done a report for <u>her</u> teacher, Mr. Sandi, but <u>she</u> was not able to choose <u>her</u> own topic. *(4)*

8. <u>It</u> had to be about <u>her</u> social studies unit. *(2)*

9. <u>Its</u> length was left up to <u>her</u>, but <u>I</u> think <u>my</u> brother learned more from researching <u>his</u> own topic. *(5)*

10. Now <u>he</u> seems like an expert on ants and <u>their</u> colonies. *(2)*

11. Mrs. McMullen said, "<u>Your</u> work on ants, Andy and Stuart, has taught <u>us</u> so much. <u>We</u> all have a greater understanding of <u>them</u>." *(4)*

Next Step: Write three sentences about an insect that you have observed. Underline the personal pronouns in each of your sentences.

1. _____

   _____

2. _____

   _____

3. _____

   _____

Pronouns and Antecedents 1

Proofreader's Guide
179, 181

The **antecedent** of the pronoun is the word the pronoun replaces. A singular antecedent takes a singular pronoun. A plural antecedent takes a plural pronoun.

■ **Singular**

A <u>student</u> should support <u>his or her</u> school team.
(The singular noun "student" is the antecedent of the singular pronouns "his" and "her.")

■ **Plural**

Team <u>members</u> must wear <u>their</u> uniforms.
(The plural noun "members" is the antecedent of the plural pronoun "their.")

Directions >> Find the antecedent for each underlined pronoun. Then draw an arrow to the antecedent. The first sentence has been done for you.

1. Each player showed <u>his or her</u> best effort.

2. Does every student have <u>his or her</u> jacket today?

3. All students must return <u>their</u> permission slips by Tuesday.

4. Students can participate if <u>they</u> fill out the correct forms.

5. Beth and Shanice brought <u>their</u> photo albums to school.

6. The table is wobbling because <u>its</u> legs are broken.

7. Jared gave his sister a present that <u>she</u> really wanted.

8. Neither Felipe nor Paul knows <u>his</u> grade on the exam.

9. My friends use <u>their</u> library cards regularly.

10. Both stores had <u>their</u> winter sales early this year.

Next Step: Write five sentences about the type of job you would like to have. Check that each pronoun and its antecedent are both singular or both plural before sharing your writing.

Pronouns and Antecedents 2

Proofreader's Guide
179, 181

The word the pronoun replaces is called an antecedent. If the antecedent is singular, the pronoun must be singular. If the antecedent is plural, the pronoun must be plural.

The boy bought his own bike.
("His" is singular because the antecedent "boy" is singular.)

The students picked up their books and went home.
("Their" is plural because the antecedent "students" is plural.)

Directions ▶ Underline the pronoun or pronouns in the sentences below and then draw an arrow to the correct antecedent in each sentence. The first sentence has been done for you.

1. The football players won their last game of the season.

2. The coach was very pleased with his squad.

3. The town was also very proud of its team.

4. By winning, the team closed out its first undefeated season in 20 years.

5. If the players win their next three games, they will be the state champions.

6. The coach had many winning seasons, yet he never won a championship.

7. The quarterback believes his team has an excellent chance to win the

   championship.

8. The students hope their team will prevail.

9. Now the players must study their opponents' weaknesses.

10. The other teams will prepare because they want to win as well.

11. We think our team is the best in the state.

Next Step: Write at least five sentences about a game or sporting event you played in or attended. Before sharing with your classmates, make sure that the pronouns match their antecedents.

Pronouns and Antecedents 3

Proofreader's Guide
179, 181

The noun the pronoun replaces is called an antecedent. If the antecedent is singular, the pronoun must be singular. If the antecedent is plural, the pronoun must be plural.

Directions ▶ Use as many of the pronouns listed below as possible in a story about a cat, dog, bird, or turtle. Underline each pronoun you use. If the pronoun has an antecedent, draw an arrow to its antecedent. Make sure each pronoun matches its antecedent. An example sentence has been done for you.

his	her	she	he	him	it	its
they	their	theirs	my	mine	our	ours

Sue needed to find her cat before dark.

_____

_____

_____

_____

_____

_____

_____

_____

_____

_____

_____

Person of a Pronoun

A first-person pronoun replaces the name of the speaker. A second-person pronoun refers to the person spoken to. Pronouns in the third person name the person or thing spoken about.

TYPE OF PRONOUN	FIRST PERSON	SECOND PERSON	THIRD PERSON
SUBJECT	I, we	you	he, she, it, they
OBJECT	me, us	you	him, her, it, them
POSSESSIVE	our, ours, my, mine	your, yours	his, her, hers, its, their, theirs

Directions ▶ Underline each personal pronoun in the following sentences. Then write "1" above each first-person pronoun, "2" above each second-person pronoun, and "3" above each third-person pronoun. The number of personal pronouns is in parentheses. The first one has been done for you.

1. <u>I</u> have <u>your</u> book, and <u>you</u> have <u>my</u> coat. *(4)*
    1   2   2   1

2. Bailey sent <u>my</u> sister and <u>me</u> a present. *(2)*
    1   1

3. <u>We</u> asked <u>her</u> to visit <u>us</u> in <u>our</u> new apartment. *(4)*
    1   3   1   1

4. When Josie and Taylor didn't see <u>us</u> on the bus, <u>they</u> thought <u>we</u> had
    1   3   1

    missed <u>it</u>. *(4)*
    3

5. Did <u>you</u> ask Lorenzo to give <u>you</u> <u>his</u> new address? *(3)*
    2   2   3

6. <u>We</u> already gave <u>him</u> <u>ours</u>. *(3)*
    1   3   1

7. Colin asked <u>you</u> and <u>me</u> to go to the movies with <u>him</u> on Saturday. *(3)*
    2   1   3

8. Either <u>my</u> sister or <u>I</u> will buy <u>your</u> ticket. *(3)*
    1   1   2

9. <u>Our</u> house is far from <u>his</u>, but <u>we</u> see <u>him</u> often anyway. *(4)*
    1   3   1   3

10. <u>I</u> know this sweater is <u>hers</u> because <u>it</u> has <u>her</u> name on <u>it</u>. *(5)*
    1   3   3   3   3

Using Verbs

A **verb** either shows action or links the subject to a noun or an adjective. The verb is the main word in the predicate part of the sentence.

■ Action Verbs

An action verb tells what the subject is doing. Strong action verbs make your writing more interesting.

Chris <u>slammed</u> the ball over the fence.

("Slammed" is an action verb.)

■ Linking Verbs

A linking verb links or connects subjects to nouns or adjectives. Some linking verbs are *is, are, was, were, am, being, been, smell, look, taste, feel, appear seem, become*.

Chris <u>is</u> a strong batter.

("Is" is a linking verb. It connects the subject "Chris" with the noun "batter.")

Directions ▶▶ Underline the verbs twice in each sentence. Write "A" above the verb if it is an action verb. Write "L" above the verb if it is a linking verb. The first one has been done for you.

1. Chris <u>belted</u> a line drive into center field. *(A)*

2. That ball <u>whizzed</u> past Jamie, the left-handed pitcher. *(A)*

3. That hit <u>sped</u> by like lightning. *(A)*

4. Chris and Jamie <u>are</u> the best players in the league. *(L)*

5. They <u>hit</u> hard, and almost every one <u>is</u> at least a two-base hit. *(A)* *(L)*

6. Chris also <u>catches</u> everything in his part of the outfield. *(A)*

7. Jamie <u>throws</u> lots of sharp-breaking curves. *(A)*

8. Jamie and Chris <u>practice</u> many times a week. *(A)*

9. They <u>become</u> better players each year. *(L)*

10. Jamie <u>looks</u> comfortable throwing the ball. *(L)*

11. Jamie and Chris <u>are</u> true baseball fans. *(L)*

■ Helping Verbs

Auxiliary or helping verbs complete the main verb. These verbs come before main verbs.

Alia <u>has given</u> some money to the Peace Corps.

(The helping verb "has" helps the main verb "given.")

> **Directions** ⟩ Helping or auxiliary verbs include "has," "had," and "have"; "do" and "did"; and forms of the verb "be" (*am, is, are, was, were, will be*). Underline the helping verb and main verb twice in each sentence.
>
> *Tip:* There can be more than one helping verb in front of the main verb. Also, sometimes other words come between the helping verb and main verb.

1. My family <u>has joined</u> the local gym.

2. We <u>have been exercising</u> for five months now.

3. Sometimes the gym <u>is crowded</u> on Saturday afternoons.

4. Last Saturday it <u>was filled</u> to its capacity.

5. I <u>had run</u> on the treadmill for 10 minutes when I <u>was asked</u> to stop.

6. Other people <u>were waiting</u> in line for the treadmill.

7. My brother <u>was using</u> the weight room at the same time.

8. He <u>has worked out</u> a lot this year.

9. He <u>had been lifting</u> weights at home.

10. He <u>does use</u> the treadmill and the pool, too.

11. My father <u>had</u> not <u>worked out</u> for several years.

12. Now he <u>is going</u> to the gym regularly.

13. My mother <u>has run</u> every day for the last 5 years.

14. She <u>has</u> always <u>had</u> lots of stamina.

Next Step: Write four sentences about an activity that interests you. Underline the verbs twice in your sentences. Make sure to underline helping verbs, too.

Types of Verbs

Action verbs tell what the subject does, did, or will do. **Linking verbs** link the subject to a noun or an adjective. **Helping verbs** are a part of the main verb.

Poison ivy <u>grows</u> as a vine or a shrub. (action)

It <u>is</u> a very common cause of allergic reaction. (linking)

Up to 50 million American <u>will develop</u> a rash from poison ivy every year. (helping)

Directions >>

In the sentences below, label the underlined verbs "A" for action verb, "L" for linking verb, and "H" for helping verb. The first one has been done for you.

1. I <u>am</u> *(L)* allergic to poison ivy; I <u>have</u> *(H)* <u>gotten</u> *(A)* a rash whenever I <u>go</u> *(A)* near it.

2. In fact, I <u>think</u> *(A)* I <u>have</u> *(H)* <u>seen</u> *(A)* poison ivy in the park near our apartment.

3. Although I <u>took</u> *(A)* a shower and <u>washed</u> *(A)* with soap, I <u>developed</u> *(A)* a rash.

4. The rash and blisters <u>are</u> *(H)* <u>bothering</u> *(A)* me all the time.

5. Sometimes, a mixture that <u>is</u> *(H)* <u>made</u> *(A)* of baking soda and water <u>helps</u> *(A)* me.

6. A poison ivy plant really <u>does</u> *(H)* <u>look</u> *(L)* quite pretty, with its shiny green leaves.

7. Poison ivy <u>will</u> *(H)* <u>produce</u> *(A)* white berries.

8. The leaves <u>have</u> *(A)* notches in them and <u>are</u> *(L)* pointy at the tips.

9. In the autumn, the leaves <u>become</u> *(L)* bright red and orange.

10. The plants <u>contain</u> *(A)* a poisonous oil.

11. If you touch the plant, you <u>could</u> *(H)* <u>get</u> *(A)* blisters.

12. Some people, however, <u>are</u> *(L)* not allergic to the plants.

13. They <u>do</u> *(H)* not <u>get</u> *(A)* itchy skin and never <u>worry</u> *(A)* about poison ivy.

Next Step: Write three sentences about something you or someone you know is allergic to. Label each verb in your sentences.

Using "Be" Verbs

A **be verb** explains whether the condition of the subject is in the past, present, or future. These verbs include *am, are, is; was, were; will be.* A *be* verb must agree with its subject in person and number.

Incorrect: **I be twelve years old.** (present)
Corrected: **I am twelve years old.** (present)

PERSON	SINGULAR	PLURAL	PRESENT SINGULAR	PRESENT PLURAL	PAST SINGULAR	FUTURE PLURAL
FIRST	I am	we are	I was	we were	I will be	we will be
SECOND	you are	you are	you were	you were	you will be	you will be
THIRD	he, she, it is	they are	he, she, it was	they were	he, she, it will be	they will be

> **Directions** In the sentences below, fill in the blanks with a correct form of the "be" verb. The first one has been done for you.

1. Jolanna _____*will be*_____ here next week.

2. LeRoy _____*was*_____ 11 years old last year.

3. Belinda, Sue, and Bianca _____*were*_____ at the mall last night.

4. I _____*am*_____ sure the bus will not leave before 8:00 a.m.

5. Although we had to wait a long time, now we _____*are*_____ ready to go.

6. Today, George _____*is*_____ confident, but you _____*are*_____ not.

7. We tried to be on time yesterday, but we _____*were*_____ late.

8. Your mother said that you _____*will be*_____ on vacation next week.

9. The dog did not leave the house because it _____*was*_____ scared.

10. You _____*were*_____ not home when I called last Sunday.

11. Keenan _____*was*_____ here two weeks ago, but Sulu _____*is*_____ here now.

12. Someone said the movie _____*is (or) was*_____ okay.

Next Step: Write six sentences using one of these "be" verbs in each: *is, will be, was, are,* and *were.* Talk with a classmate about your sentences.

Modal Verbs 1

A **modal verb** is a word that is like a helping verb. It works together with the main verb to express meaning.

Common Modal Verbs		
can	must	will
could	have to	would
might	have got to	may
	ought to	

I might have a pizza party.

(In this sentence "might" is a modal and "have" is the main verb.)

Would you help me?

(In this sentence "would" is a modal and "help" is the main verb.)

Directions ➤ Circle the modal verbs, and underline the main verbs twice in each sentence below. (Notice that the modals and the main verbs are not always next to each other.) The first one has been done for you.

1. I (might) celebrate my birthday with a huge pizza party.

2. I (may) talk to my parents about my plans.

3. They probably (will) agree to the idea, but I (must) ask them first.

4. (Would) you help me with the invitations?

5. I (can) help you on Thursday after school.

6. My sister (may) have some ideas about decorations.

7. There (ought to) be good music for a great party.

8. (Could) you loan me some of your CD's?

9. You (may) borrow any of them, and I (can) bring my CD player, too.

10. I (have got to) decide on a time for the party.

Next Step: Use modal verbs to write three sentences that ask permission or make a request.

Modal Verbs 2

In this activity, you will practice working with modal verbs, which help the main verb express meaning.

Directions ❯ Below is a list of modal verbs. Write six sentences. In each sentence use a different modal verb from the list.

would	ought to	might	must
can	may	will	have to

1. _I might want to see a movie this weekend._

2. _My sister ought to save more money._

3. _My brother and I have to clean the garage for Dad._

4. _My English teacher may show a video of the last book we read._

5. _You must stand in line for hours to get tickets to the concert._

6. _I would go to a show with you if I didn't have to baby-sit for my aunt._

Next Step: Write three more sentences about something you should do or would like to do. In each sentence use a different modal verb. Share your work with a classmate to check your sentences.

Helping Verbs 1

A **helping verb** works with the main verb to express time, action, and meaning. Helping verbs come before main verbs, but other words can come between them. These words can be adverbs (*not, really, usually, often*) or nouns or pronouns (*you, she, it, James, children*).

I am going to the library.

(The verb "am" helps state continuous action.)

I have always liked my books on petrified forests.

(The verb "have" helps state an action that started in the past and is still going on.)

Common Helping Verbs		
am, are	do	have
is, was	does	has
were, will	did	had

Directions ▶ Circle each helping verb, and underline each main verb twice. The first one has been done for you.

1. (Do) you <u>know</u> about petrified forests?

2. A petrified forest (is) <u>composed</u> of very old tree trunks.

3. These tree trunks (have) <u>turned</u> to stone.

4. They (were) <u>buried</u> in mud or sand many years ago.

5. Over time, underground water (had) <u>filled</u> the empty tree trunks.

6. Hard minerals from the water (have) <u>replaced</u> the wood in the tree trunks.

7. Some of these minerals, like iron and manganese, (have) <u>given</u> the grayish trees spots of bright yellow, red, and purple.

8. Petrified forests (are) <u>found</u> in several states.

9. The most famous petrified forest (is) <u>located</u> in northern Arizona.

Next Step: Write three sentences about something you have learned in science or some other class that interests you. Use helping verbs in each sentence.

Helping Verbs 2

Some helping verbs include forms of "have" (*has, have, had*), forms of "do" (*do, does, did*), and forms of "be" (*is, am, was, were,* and so on). Helping verbs give more information about the action or the time of the main verb. *Note:* A word that may be a helping verb in one sentence may be a main verb in another.

Rodney did not go to school yesterday.

(The helping verb "did" helps state past action.)

Does she remember the song?

(The helping verb "does" helps state present action.)

Directions ➤ Fill in the blank in each sentence below with one of the following helping verbs. You will use some verbs twice. The first sentence has been done for you.

are	is	was	were	do	has	have

1. My cousin _____*was*_____ born in Texas.

2. He _____*has*_____ lived there all his life.

3. Many of my relatives _____*were*_____ born there long ago.

4. I _____*do*_____ want to visit my cousin this summer.

5. When I go to Texas, my brother and sister _____*are*_____ coming with me.

6. We _____*have*_____ asked a neighbor to take care of our dog.

7. Buttons _____*is*_____ playing in the yard right now.

8. Now he _____*is*_____ chasing his tail.

9. _____*Are*_____ you packing enough warm-weather clothes?

10. Please _____*do*_____ send us a postcard!

Next Step: Helping verbs also can be main verbs. Choose three helping verbs from the list above. Write a sentence using each as a main verb.

Two-Word Verbs

This activity will give you practice identifying two-words verbs. You usually do not separate the words of a two-word verb.

Incorrect: **They called the meeting off.**
Corrected: **They called off the meeting.**

PROGRAM NOTE
CALLED OFF

> **Directions** Fill in the blank in each sentence with one of the two-word verbs below. The first one has been done for you.

take down	shut off	hand in	write down
pick out	cross out	put away	talk over
call off	try on	hand out	take part

1. The principal said, "___Take down___ the stage."

2. Once we finished, he said we should ___shut off___ the lights.

3. He will ___call off___ the concert for this afternoon.

4. The choir director will ___pick out___ new music for next month's concert.

5. Please ___put away___ the chairs.

6. ___Hand out___ these schedules to the new students.

7. Choir members must ___try on___ the new robes.

8. ___Write down___ the names of the choir members in this notebook.

9. Just ___cross out___ your misspellings and write the correct name above.

10. After finishing the assignment, ___hand in___ your papers.

> **Directions** Write your own sentences for the two remaining two-word verbs.

1. *The class talked over hurricane evacuation plans.*

2. *Students will take part in a practice evacuation.*

leave out	pick out	points out	filled out	get on	get off
get out	shut off	put down	looked up	call up	

1 The teacher announced last week that today we would go on a field

2 trip. Our parents or guardians to ___*filled out*___ permission slips. They could

3 not ___*leave out*___ any information. Because it is late in the school year and

4 all of our work is done, we are going to a baseball game. The teacher and

5 other chaperones just said we should ___*get on*___ the bus. This is going to

6 be great!

7   The bus ride took about an hour, and the driver found a great parking

8 space. He ___*shut off*___ the engine. Now we can ___*get off*___ the bus and

9 go into the stadium. There sure are a lot of people in the stands today. How

10 did all these people ___*get out*___ of work? Before the game starts, we must

11 ___*pick out*___ the food we want. I have decided to buy a hot dog and soda.

12   So far the game has been pretty exciting. I ___*looked up*___ the name of

13 this batter. I ___*put down*___ my soft drink and read about his batting average.

14 A friend of mine ___*points out*___ his favorite player, and we argue over which

15 player has had the best season so far. We win the game, and it's time to go

16 home. I will ___*call up*___ my friend to tell him all about our day at the ball

17 park!

Next Step: Write a sentence for each of the following two-word verbs:

filled up ___*Rhonda filled up the last page in her journal.*___

gave back ___*Students gave back the special pencils after the test.*___

Simple Verb Tenses

A verb in the **present tense** tells about an action that is happening at the present time or that happens regularly. A verb in the **past tense** tells about an action that happened in the past. A verb in the **future tense** tells about an action that will happen.

- ■ **Present Tense**

  Al <u>attends</u> middle school.

  (The action "attends" is happening now and regularly.)

- ■ **Past Tense**

  Last year, he <u>attended</u> elementary school.

  (The action "attended" happened at a specific time in the past.)

- ■ **Future Tense**

  After eighth grade, he <u>will attend</u> high school.

  (The action "will attend" will happen in the future.)

Directions ▶ Tell something about what you do now, what you did, and what you will do, by completing the following sentences.

1. *(Use a present-tense verb.)* Right now, I _write articles for the school_

paper.

_____

2. *(Use a past-tense verb.)* Last year, I _wrote a special feature about our_

school mascot.

_____

3. *(Use a future-tense verb.)* In 10 years, I _will write for a local TV news_

channel, I hope.

_____

Underline with two lines each verb in the following sentences. Underline any helping verbs as well. Then write the tense of the verb on the line. The first one has been done for you.

**present** 1. Regan's favorite subject <u>is</u> art.

present 2. She <u>enjoys</u> drawing and painting.

past 3. Her grandmother <u>was</u> an artist.

past 4. Jussara's parents <u>were born</u> in Portugal.

future 5. Jussara <u>will go</u> to Portugal next summer.

future 6. Sumit <u>will celebrate</u> his birthday next week.

past 7. The United States <u>fought</u> the British during the American Revolution.

future 8. When <u>will</u> you <u>finish</u> your report?

present 9. I <u>have</u> all my materials ready now.

past 10. Tamar really <u>wanted</u> a part in the play.

present 11. Sophia, Olivia, and Bolivia <u>are</u> triplets.

present 12. They really <u>look</u> a lot alike.

past 13. Roger <u>brought</u> his new CD to school.

past 14. We <u>left</u> school early yesterday.

past 15. Suleika <u>wrote</u> a letter to the principal about our field trip.

future 16. We <u>will go</u> on our field trip in April.

Next Step: Write three sentences about a goal that you have now, one that you had in the past, and one that you expect to have in the future. Use the correct verb tenses in your sentences.

Simple and Perfect Tenses

Verb tenses indicate time. **Simple tenses** show that an event happens in the present, past, or future. The **perfect tenses** show special relationships between events and time.

- **Present Perfect Tense** expresses an action that started in the past and is still going on.

  Alfonso <u>has</u> always <u>enjoyed</u> mysteries.

  (Use "has" or "have" in front of a past-tense verb to form this perfect tense.)

- **Past Perfect Tense** expresses an action that started and finished in the past.

  Saki <u>had moved</u> his bike under the bridge before the storm.

  (Use "had" in front of a past-tense verb to form this perfect tense.)

- **Future Perfect Tense** expresses an action that will begin and end at a specific time in the future.

  By Friday, they <u>will have practiced</u> for six hours.

  (Use "will have" in front of a past-tense verb to form this perfect tense.)

> **Directions**   For each verb that follows, write three sentences using the tense that is asked for. The first one has been done for you.

1. want

I want that cup.

(present tense)

I wanted the green bowl.

(past tense)

Ann has wanted a new bike for several years.

(present perfect tense: an action that started in the past and is still going on)

2. walk

Tai walked through the park.

(past tense)

The girls will walk home after gymnastics.

(future tense)

The team had walked five miles by sundown.

(past perfect tense: an action that started and finished in the past)

3. work

I worked five days last month.

(past tense)

I will work in the school library next week.

(future tense)

I have worked there for at least three months.

(present perfect tense)

4. bake

Lana bakes cupcakes for her mom.

(present tense)

Sophie had baked a prizewinning cake.

(past perfect tense)

By Tuesday Sarah will have baked a pie for the class.

(future perfect tense)

5. verb of your choice _____

_____

(past tense)

_____

(future tense)

_____

(past perfect tense)

Next Step: Use the correct perfect tense of the verb "finish."

1. I always _____ *have finished* _____ my homework on time. *(present perfect)*

2. By last Thursday, Matt _____ *had finished* _____ his report. *(past perfect)*

3. I _____ *will have finished* _____ my homework by dinnertime. *(future perfect)*

Irregular Verbs 1

Proofreader's Guide
183-184

Irregular verbs are verbs that do not end in *ed* either in the past tense, or when they are used with *has, have,* or *had.* Instead, the whole word usually changes. Carefully read this list of irregular verbs several times.

Present: I **begin** my day at dawn.

Past: I **began** an after-school job last week.

Past Participle: I **had begun** looking for a job last summer.

PRESENT TENSE	PAST TENSE	PAST PARTICIPLE	PRESENT TENSE	PAST TENSE	PAST PARTICIPLE
begin	began	begun	meet	met	met
do	did	done	see	saw	seen
find	found	found	speak	spoke	spoken
give	gave	given	swim	swam	swum
go	went	gone	write	wrote	written

Directions ▶ Carefully study the irregular verbs above. Cover them with a sheet of paper. Then write the principal parts of the verbs listed below. Check your work after you have finished.

Present Tense	Past Tense	Past Participle
begin	*began*	*begun*
do	*did*	*done*
find	*found*	*found*
give	*gave*	*given*
go	*went*	*gone*
meet	*met*	*met*
see	*saw*	*seen*
speak	*spoke*	*spoken*
write	*wrote*	*written*

PRESENT TENSE	PAST TENSE	PAST PARTICIPLE	PRESENT TENSE	PAST TENSE	PAST PARTICIPLE
be (am, is, are)	was, were	been	pay	paid	paid
break	broke	broken	run	ran	run
burst	burst	burst	send	sent	sent
choose	chose	chosen	stand	stood	stood
drive	drove	driven	teach	taught	taught
fly	flew	flown	think	thought	thought
grow	grew	grown	bring	brought	brought

	Present Tense	Past Tense	Past Participle
1.	be (am, is, are)	was, were	been
2.	break	broke	broken
3.	burst	burst	burst
4.	choose	chose	chosen
5.	drive	drove	driven
6.	fly	flew	flown
7.	grow	grew	grown
8.	pay	paid	paid
9.	run	ran	run
10.	send	sent	sent
11.	stand	stood	stood
12.	teach	taught	taught
13.	think	thought	thought
14.	bring	brought	brought

Next Step: Write five sentences about what you did last weekend. Use at least one irregular verb in each sentence.

Irregular Verbs 2

Proofreader's Guide
183-184

Some irregular verbs do not change their spelling in the past tense or in combination with *have, has,* or *had.* See the following chart:

Yesterday Jon <u>spread</u> butter on his toast.

Sometimes John <u>has spread</u> chocolate frosting on graham crackers for dessert.

PRESENT TENSE	PAST TENSE	PAST PARTICIPLE	PRESENT TENSE	PAST TENSE	PAST PARTICIPLE
cost	cost	cost	put	put	put
cut	cut	cut	read	read	read
hit	hit	hit	set	set	set
let	let	let	spread	spread	spread

Add an *s* to any of the present-tense verbs listed above to use with third-person singular subjects.

Jon <u>spreads</u> peanut butter on his crackers.

 **Directions** ▶ For each verb that follows, write three sentences using the tense indicated in parentheses. The first one has been done for you.

1. hit

Alicia and Su hit tennis balls.

(*present tense*)

Alonzo hit a pothole on his bike yesterday.

(*past tense*)

The temperature had hit an all-time record low.

(*past perfect tense*)

2. put

Franco puts his uniform in the closet.

(*present tense*)

Salvatore put the game away last Friday.

(*past tense*)

Ricky has put his shirts in the drawer.

(*present perfect tense*)

3. cost

Those gloves cost five dollars.

(present tense)

The socks cost him two dollars.

(past tense)

Jeans have cost as much as forty dollars a pair.

(present perfect tense)

4. read

I currently read a book a month.

(present tense)

I read my first 500-page book last summer.

(past tense)

Elaine had read a great story about a deaf-and-blind couple.

(past perfect tense)

5. set

Hakiu sets the cement blocks on the pavement.

(present tense)

Hiro set the boards on the blocks yesterday.

(past tense)

I will have set the chairs in place by three o'clock.

(future perfect tense)

6. verb of your choice _____

_____

(present tense)

_____

(past tense)

_____

(future perfect tense)

Next Step: The irregular verb "read" has the same spelling in all three principal parts, but its pronunciation is different in the present tense. In the present tense, it has a long "e," as in "reed." In the past tense and in the past participle, it has a short "e," as in "red." Write three sentences using all three principal parts of "read." Then read your sentences aloud.

Irregular Verbs 3

Regular verbs form their past tense and past participles by adding *ed* to the verb (*walk—walked*). Most irregular verbs form their past tenses and past participles by changing their spelling.

Directions ▷ In each of the following sentences, underline the irregular verb twice. Write its past tense and past participle on the lines following the sentence. (Remember that the past participle form is used with the helping verbs "have," "has," or "had.") The first one has been done for you.

Present Tense	Past Tense	Past Participle
1. They <u>do</u> good work.	*did*	*done*
2. We <u>come</u> here often.	*came*	*come*
3. The birds <u>fly</u> south.	*flew*	*flown*
4. The phone <u>rings</u> often.	*rang*	*rung*
5. Marika <u>leads</u> the way.	*led*	*led*
6. She <u>meets</u> her relatives.	*met*	*met*
7. You <u>pay</u> Erik his salary.	*paid*	*paid*
8. Petra <u>runs</u> to school fast.	*ran*	*run*
9. He <u>spends</u> all his money.	*spent*	*spent*
10. I <u>swim</u> every day at the pool.	*swam*	*swum*
11. I <u>choose</u> to swim at 5:00 p.m.	*chose*	*chosen*
12. I <u>bring</u> my own towel.	*brought*	*brought*

Next Step: Write two sentences, one using the past tense and another using the past participle of the verb "throw."

_____

_____

_____

Irregular Verb Review

Complete this review to practice using the different forms of irregular verbs. Most irregular verbs change their spelling in the past tense or in combination with *have, has,* or *had*; but some irregular verbs do not change their spelling.

> **Directions** ⟩ Correct each underlined irregular verb below by writing the correct form above it. The first one has been done for you.

       read
1. Octavia has already <u>readed</u> "The Tell-Tale Heart" several times.

      wrote
2. Leonard Bernstein <u>writed</u> the music for *West Side Story*.

  saw
3. Jessica <u>seen</u> the movie *West Side Story* four times.

    thought
4. She <u>thinked</u> the movie's music was great.

    bought
5. She even <u>buyed</u> the CD with her own money.

   did
6. Forrest <u>done</u> his homework to prepare for the test.

  took
7. Mike <u>taked</u> a lot of books home from school today.

   chose
8. I think he <u>choosed</u> to do some work for extra credit.

   gave   *written*
9. Mrs. Lowry <u>gived</u> the class a report that could be <u>wrote</u> at home.

   taught   *sent*
10. She also <u>teached</u> us to use the Internet, and we <u>sended</u> some e-mail.

   fell   *broke*
11. When Bart <u>falled</u> off his chair, he <u>breaked</u> his glasses.

    cost
12. His new glasses <u>costed</u> a lot of money.

Next Step: Write three sentences, using one irregular verb in each.

_____

_____

_____

Using Adjectives

Adjectives modify nouns and pronouns. Adjectives answer questions about the words they modify. They can tell *what kind* (a *young* girl), *which one* (*that* story), and *how many* (*five* people). Adjectives usually come before the words they describe. They are never plural. The words *a, an,* and *the* are special adjectives called *articles.*

Directions ▶ Underline the adjectives in the following sentences. For this exercise, do not underline the adjectives "a," "an," or "the." (The number of adjectives is given in parentheses.) The first sentence has been done for you.

1. The story of Madame C. J. Walker is an <u>interesting</u> one about a <u>full</u> life. *(2)*

2. Her <u>given</u> name was Sarah Breedlove. *(1)*

3. She was born to <u>poor</u> parents in <u>rural</u> Louisiana in 1867. *(2)*

4. Sarah attended only <u>three</u> months of school in her <u>whole</u> life. *(2)*

5. When her parents died, she married because she had no <u>real</u> home. *(1)*

6. A <u>few</u> years later, she went north to a <u>big</u> city, St. Louis, with her <u>young</u> daughter and washed clothes for a job. *(3)*

7. She earned <u>little</u> money, but she saved <u>those</u> earnings and later developed a <u>great</u> <u>new</u> product. *(4)*

8. She lost <u>some</u> hair because of <u>bad</u> food and <u>insufficient</u> sleep. *(3)*

9. A <u>wise</u> friend recommended a <u>hair</u> tonic of <u>coconut</u> oil and sulfur, with <u>other</u> ingredients to give it a <u>flowery</u> smell. *(5)*

10. Madame Walker experimented with <u>other</u> ingredients to develop her <u>own</u> formula to condition <u>unhealthy</u> scalps. *(3)*

11. She hired <u>other</u> women to sell <u>these</u> <u>special</u> products. *(3)*

12. Madame Walker was one of the <u>first</u> <u>African American</u> millionaires. *(2)*

Forms of Adjectives 1

We use adjectives in three different forms: positive, comparative, and superlative. Each form is shown below.

■ **Positive** adjectives describe a noun without comparing it to another noun.

Shanti is the <u>young</u> daughter of Bill Hong.
That paint is <u>expensive</u>.

■ **Comparative** adjectives compare two people, places, things, or ideas. Add *er* to most one-syllable words. Most adjectives with two or more syllables use *more* or *less* to form the comparative.

Shanti is <u>younger</u> than her brother Ravi.
The paint is <u>more expensive</u> than I remember. *(or)* **less expensive**

■ **Superlative** adjectives compare three or more people, places, things, or ideas. Add *est* to most one-syllable words. Most adjectives with two or more syllables use *most* or *least* to form the superlative.

Shanti is the <u>youngest</u> student in her class.
It is the <u>most expensive</u> paint I have ever used. *(or)* **least expensive**

Directions ⟩ For each of the following sentences, write the correct form of the adjective on the line. The first one has been done for you.

1. Jared is _____*older*_____ than you. *(old)*

2. I think he is _____*younger*_____ than my brother, however. *(young)*

3. Walking is the __*least (or) most popular*__ exercise of all. *(popular)*

4. Some of the exercises are __*less (or) more difficult*__ than others. *(difficult)*

5. Doing chin-ups is the __*least (or) most difficult*__ for me. *(difficult)*

6. This gym is not the _____*largest*_____ in the city. *(large)*

7. The one across town is _____*larger*_____ than this gym, I think. *(large)*

Forms of Adjectives 2

Here is some practice using the comparative and superlative forms of adjectives.

Directions ▶ Read the following sentences and cross out the wrong form of the adjective. Then write the correct form above that word. The first sentence has been done for you.

better
1. Billy's scraped knee is ~~gooder~~ than it was yesterday.

best
2. Sue does the ~~bestest~~ work in the class.

faster
3. Frank is a ~~more fast~~ runner than Kai.

worse   *worse*
4. Samone's eyesight just seems to get ~~worser~~ and ~~worser~~.

taller
5. Luis is even ~~more tall~~ than Juan is!

easier
6. Cats are ~~more easy~~ to take care of than dogs.

heavier
7. The man bought the SUV because it was ~~heaviest~~ than the car he owned.

least
8. Fulyana is the ~~leastest~~ likely of anyone in her family to get homesick.

cheapest
9. Neil bought the ~~cheaper~~ shirt he could find.

dry
10. The clothes were not very ~~driest~~.

most
11. Rita got a prize because she sold the ~~mostest~~ tickets for the class play.

youngest
12. Fernando is the ~~younger~~ in his class.

better
13. Kyoko's essay is ~~more good~~ than mine.

happy
14. Angel danced because she was so ~~happiest~~.

younger
15. Manuel is the ~~youngest~~ of my two sons.

Next Step: In your own words, write the story of *Goldilocks and the Three Bears* (or another children's story). Use as many positive, comparative, and superlative forms of adjectives as you can. Compare stories.

Identify the words or phrases below as "positive," "comparative," or "superlative." Then write a sentence using the word or phrase. The first one has been done for you.

Answers will vary.

1. better ____comparative____

This movie is better than the last one I saw.

2. least important ____superlative____

The broken glass was the least important problem.

3. worse ____comparative____

The cut on his hand seems to be worse today than yesterday.

4. pretty ____positive____

Jolene is a pretty girl.

5. colder ____comparative____

The weather will turn colder on Saturday.

6. most amazing ____superlative____

The gymnast did the most amazing jump at the Olympics.

7. soft ____positive____

The baby is wrapped in a soft blanket.

8. slowest ____superlative____

A snail must be the slowest animal in the world.

9. more unusual ____comparative____

The students thought this story was more unusual than the last one they had read.

Next Step: Exchange papers with a classmate and discuss your answers.

Forms of Adjectives 3

Some adjectives, such as *many* and *good*, use a completely different word in their comparative and superlative forms. Study the chart below to learn about specific forms of adjectives.

Special Forms of Adjectives		
POSITIVE	COMPARATIVE	SUPERLATIVE
good	better	best
bad	worse	worst
many	more	most
little	less	least

Note: Do not use *more* or *most* (*less* or *least*) with forms of *good* and *bad*.

Directions ⟩⟩ Underline the correct form of the adjective in parentheses in each sentence. The first one has been done for you.

1. Taylor's grades are (*good* / *better*) than Haley's.

2. Ynez read (*more* / *most*) books than Cameron.

3. Felicia studies the (*more* / *most*) of anyone in the class.

4. Dustin has a (*bad* / *worst*) cold again.

5. He thinks it is the (*worse* / *worst*) cold he has ever had.

6. Dustin has very (*little* / *least*) energy when he is sick.

7. Today he has eaten (*less* / *least*) than yesterday.

8. I hope that he doesn't get any (*worse* / *worst*) than he is today.

9. He has caught (*many* / *more*) colds than his brother has.

10. Dustin is my (*better* / *best*) friend.

Directions ⟩⟩ Write a sentence in which you use the positive, comparative, and superlative forms of one of the adjectives in the box above.

Adjectives **133**

Write three sentences for each of the adjectives below. Use the *positive form* of the adjective in the first sentence, the *comparative form* in the second sentence, and the *superlative form* in the third sentence. *Answers will vary.*

1. **rich**

   (positive) _She is rich._

   (comparative) _I believe she is richer than the senator._

   _____

   (superlative) _Some say she is the richest person in the state._

   _____

2. **interesting**

   (positive) _The teacher gave an interesting lecture today._

   (comparative) _Phil's science project is more interesting than mine._

   _____

   (superlative) _The golden retriever proved to be the most interesting_

   animal in the pet store.

3. **simple**

   (positive) _The math problem is simple._

   (comparative) _Today's math problem is simpler than yesterday's._

   _____

   (superlative) _This is the simplest test we have had all year._

   _____

Next Step: Write three sentences comparing two or more different activities or stores. Use as many special forms of adjectives as you can. Then exchange sentences with a classmate and check each other's work.

Using Adverbs

Adverbs modify verbs, adjectives, or other adverbs. The four types of adverbs are adverbs of time (telling *when, how often,* or *how long)*, place (telling *where, to where,* or *from where*), manner (telling *how* something is done), and degree (telling *how much* or *how little*). Many adverbs end with *ly*.

- **Time** It was <u>late</u>.
- **Place** He went <u>away</u>.
- **Manner** She slept <u>soundly</u>.
- **Degree** It was <u>quite</u> humid.

Directions >> Place the adverbs listed below in their proper places on the chart. There are five adverbs of each type. (Two adverbs have been charted for you.)

today	noisily	later	monthly	yesterday
under	well	somewhat	sweetly	nearby
angrily	down	here	beyond	thoroughly
very	more	swiftly	before	rather

Time *(when)*	**Place** *(where)*	**Manner** *(how)*	**Degree** *(how much)*
yesterday	nearby	swiftly	more
today	under	well	thoroughly
later	down	angrily	rather
monthly	beyond	noisily	somewhat
before	here	sweetly	very

Directions >> Add three more adverbs to each category in the chart above.

On the following lines, write six sentences, using different types of adverbs. The first one has been done for you.

Answers will vary.

1. *(adverb of time)*

   The custodian will clean the floor later.

2. *(adverb of place)*

   The teacher set her books there.

3. *(adverb of manner)*

   The student quickly wrote his name on his paper.

4. *(adverb of degree)*

   Stefan is very excited about the big game.

5. *(adverb of time)*

   I will write a letter to Grandpa tomorrow.

6. *(adverb of place)*

   Stephanie fell down.

7. *(adverb of manner)*

   My uncle read the story dramatically.

Next Step: Write three sentences about a movie or television entertainer that you like. Use the four types of adverbs in your writing. Share your work with a classmate and discuss your choices.

Forms of Adverbs

Like adjectives, adverbs have positive, comparative, and superlative forms.

■ **Positive**

In the positive form, the adverb does not make a comparison.

Alejandro runs fast.
Luisa exercises frequently.

■ **Comparative**

The comparative is formed by adding *er* to one-syllable adverbs or the word *more* or *less* before longer adverbs. (If an adverb ends in *y*, change the *y* to *i* before adding *er*.)

Alejandro runs faster than his brother.
Luisa exercises more frequently than I do.

■ **Superlative**

The superlative is formed by adding *est* to one-syllable adverbs or *most* or *least* before longer adverbs. (If an adverb ends in *y*, change the *y* to *i* before adding *est*.)

Alejandro runs fastest during a race.
Of all her friends, Luisa exercises most frequently.

> **Directions** ⟩ Rewrite each sentence below twice, using the correct form of the underlined adverb. The first one has been done for you.

1. (*positive*) Trayce's bus arrived early.

   (*comparative*) _Trayce's bus arrived earlier today than yesterday._

   (*superlative*) _Considering the whole week, Trayce's bus arrived earliest on_

   Monday.

2. (*positive*) _Clarissa acts calmly around snakes._

   _____

   (*comparative*) Clarissa acts more calmly than Ramon around snakes.

   (*superlative*) _Between spiders, snakes, and mice, Clarissa acts most_

   calmly around snakes.

3. (*positive*) _Daryl skates gracefully._

(*comparative*) _Daryl skates more gracefully than Cheryl._

(*superlative*) Of all the people on the rink, Daryl skates <u>most gracefully</u>.

4. (*positive*) Ian gets up <u>late</u>.

(*comparative*) _Ian gets up later than his brother._

(*superlative*) _Of all his cousins, Ian gets up latest._

5. (*positive adverb of your choice*) _____

(*comparative*) _____

(*superlative*) _____

Next Step: Write a sports review of a game or competition in which you describe the performances of the athletes. Use as many positive, comparative, and superlative forms of adverbs as you can. Exchange papers with a classmate and compare your sports-page reviews.

Using Interjections

Proofreader's Guide
152, 186

An **interjection** is a word or a group of words that expresses strong emotion or surprise. An interjection often appears as part of the dialogue in a story or play. Use an exclamation point or a comma to separate an interjection from the rest of the sentence.

Ugh! This milk is sour.

Well, we should take it back.

Directions » Use a different interjection from the box below to fill in each blank in the following sentences. The first sentence has been done for you.

Hey	Okay	Yeah	Wow	No kidding	Really
Listen	Uh-oh	No way	Well	Fantastic	Sure

Answers may vary.

1. My sister yelled. "_____*Hey*_____! Answer the phone!"

2. "_____*Okay*_____," I said, "but it's always for you anyway."

3. _____*Well*_____, it usually is! She wastes a lot of time on the phone, and here's what I hear her say.

4. "I don't believe it. _____*No kidding*_____!"

5. "_____*Yeah*_____! That's what I thought."

6. "That sounds great. _____*Fantastic*_____!"

7. "_____*Wow*_____! I can't believe it."

8. "_____*Really*_____! That's hilarious!"

9. "_____*Uh-oh*_____, I almost forgot that."

10. "I have great news. _____*Listen*_____!"

Next Step: Write your own telephone dialogue using interjections. Work with a partner if you wish. Read your finished dialogue out loud.

Using Prepositions

Prepositions are words that show position or direction. They introduce prepositional phrases. The chart below lists some common prepositions.

aboard	around	beside	from	of	through	up
about	at	between	in	on	to	with
after	before	by	into	over	toward	
against	below	during	like	past	under	
along	beneath	for	near	since	until	

> **Directions** Underline the prepositions in the following sentences. The number of prepositions in each sentence is shown in parentheses. The first sentence has been done for you.

1. Jesse Owens once said, "In America, anybody can become somebody." *(1)*

2. United States track star Jesse Owens was born with few advantages. *(1)*

3. He was born in Oakville, Alabama, in 1915, the grandson of former slaves. *(3)*

4. In college at Ohio State University, he set several track records. *(2)*

5. After working and studying, he spent much of his time on the track practicing. *(3)*

6. During the 1936 Olympic Games in Berlin, Germany, Owens secured a place in history for himself. *(4)*

7. Germany was under the control of the dictator Adolf Hitler. *(2)*

8. He tried blocking African Americans and Jews from the Olympics. *(1)*

9. From the start, the United States took a stand against Hitler's ideas. *(2)*

10. Owens broke several world records in track and won four gold medals for the United States. *(2)*

Using Prepositional Phrases

A **prepositional phrase** includes a preposition, the object of the preposition (a noun or pronoun), and any words that modify the object.

Prepositional phrases work like adjectives or adverbs because they modify a part of the sentence. The parts of the following prepositional phrases are labeled:

on the muddy river
(The word "on" is a preposition, "the" and "muddy" are adjectives, and "river" is a noun acting as the object of the preposition.)

near a big fence
(The word "near" is a preposition, "a" and "big" are adjectives, and "fence" is a noun acting as the object of the preposition.)

for them
(The word "for" is a preposition, and "them" is a pronoun acting as the object of the preposition.)

from a fairly small town
(The word "from" is a preposition, "a" and "small" are adjectives, "fairly" is an adverb, and "town" is a noun acting as the object of the preposition.)

Directions > Write a sentence using each prepositional phrase above. The first sentence has been done for you.

1. *The boat floated on the muddy river.*

2. *Jorge remembered that the abandoned car was near a big fence.*

3. *The school bought band uniforms for them.*

4. *Adam felt lost in the city because he was from a fairly small town.*

Write three sentences using prepositional phrases of your own choosing. Underline the prepositional phrases in your sentences. Here is an example:

I put my backpack <u>on the blue chair</u> and then sat down.

1. _She ran quickly <u>around the track</u>._

2. _The sun finally broke <u>through the clouds</u>._

3. _Trying to show off, Bill fell <u>off the wall</u> and broke his arm._

Directions Change the underlined preposition in the sample sentence below as many times as possible. One change has been done for you. (Continue this exercise on your own paper.)

Thea walked <u>through</u> the park. _Answers will vary._

Thea walked <u>around</u> the park.

Thea walked <u>into</u> the park.

Thea walked <u>by</u> the park.

Thea walked <u>past</u> the park.

Thea walked <u>toward</u> the park.

Thea walked <u>from</u> the park.

Thea walked <u>in</u> the park.

Thea walked <u>near</u> the park.

Thea walked <u>to</u> the park.

Next Step: Exchange your work with a partner. Who has used the most prepositions in sentences that make sense?

Using Coordinating Conjunctions 1

Coordinating conjunctions connect two or more equal sentence parts: words, phrases, or clauses.

I enjoy studying animals <u>and</u> geography.

(The conjunction "and" connects two words.)

Did Mr. Zold study wildlife in South Africa <u>or</u> in Zimbabwe?

(The conjunction "or" connects two prepositional phrases.)

He loves all wildlife, <u>but</u> he especially likes apes and monkeys.

(The conjunction "but" connects two independent clauses.)

Directions ▶ Use one of the coordinating conjunctions listed below to fill in each blank in the following sentences.

and	but	or	so	yet

Answers may vary.

1. Do you know some of the differences between apes _____*and*_____ monkeys?

2. Monkeys have long tails, _____*but*_____ apes have none.

3. Gorillas _____*and*_____ chimpanzees are apes.

4. Monkeys live in trees, _____*but*_____ apes spend more time on the ground.

5. Both monkeys _____*and*_____ apes eat mostly fruits and vegetables.

6. The feet of apes have thumbs instead of big toes, _____*so*_____ they can use their feet as humans use hands.

7. Ape's arms are longer than our arms, _____*but*_____ their legs are shorter.

8. Monkeys are smaller than apes, _____*yet*_____ they have similar feet.

9. Monkeys express themselves by making different noises, such as screaming to show either anger _____*or*_____ fear.

10. Monkeys usually eat just after sunrise _____*or*_____ just before sundown.

Using Coordinating Conjunctions 2

Proofreader's Guide
152, 186

Coordinating conjunctions (*and, but, or, nor, for, so, yet*) can be used to connect two simple sentences (clauses) to create a compound sentence. A comma is always used before the coordinating conjunction in a compound sentence.

Directions ⟩ Connect each pair of simple sentences. Use a comma and the coordinating conjunction in parentheses. The first one has been done for you. *Answers may vary.*

1. Milk was on sale at the market. My mom bought an extra gallon. (*so*)

   Milk was on sale at the market, so my mom bought an extra gallon.

2. Eliana studied for the exam. She did not do as well as she had hoped. (*yet*)

   Eliana studied for the exam, yet she did not do as well as she had hoped.

3. Luisa runs every morning. She usually takes her dog. (*and*)

   Luisa runs every morning, and she usually takes her dog.

4. We may take a trip to Seattle. We may go to San Francisco. (*or*)

   We may take a trip to Seattle, or we may go to San Francisco.

5. The tire pressure was too high. Claude still added more air. (*but*)

   The tire pressure was too high, but Claude still added more air.

6. We added two eggs to the mix. We beat it with the electric mixer. (*and*)

   We added two eggs to the mix, and we beat it with the electric mixer.

Using Subordinating Conjunctions 1

Subordinating conjunctions join two clauses to form a complex sentence. The subordinating conjunction is always used at the beginning of the dependent clause in a complex sentence.

Common Subordinating Conjunctions

after	as though	in order that	unless
although	because	since	until
as	before	so	when
as if	even though	so that	where
as long as	if	though	while

Directions ▷ Underline the subordinating conjunction in each of the following sentences. The first sentence has been done for you.

1. My family will travel to Florida <u>because</u> my grandparents live there.

2. <u>Although</u> we went last summer, we want to go again.

3. We didn't see everything we wanted to see <u>while</u> we were there.

4. Our grandparents took us to the beach <u>since</u> they live nearby.

5. My sister likes to build sand castles <u>when</u> we are at the beach.

6. My brother plays in the waves <u>until</u> it's time to leave.

7. I like to look for shells <u>even though</u> I don't collect them.

8. <u>If</u> I find some that aren't broken, I am happy.

9. <u>Before</u> we leave for the beach, we fill a cooler with sandwiches.

10. <u>After</u> swimming for an hour, I am very hungry.

11. I eat my sandwich <u>though</u> it is too early for lunch.

12. <u>Unless</u> it rains, we always want to go back the next day.

Using Subordinating Conjunctions 2

Here is more practice using subordinating conjunctions.

Directions ⟩ Choose subordinating conjunctions from the chart to complete the sentences. You may use them more than once.

after	when	so that	while	as though
if	as if	as long as	because	although
where	since	before	until	though

1. _Although (or) Though_ Australia is a big island, it is also a continent.

2. Australia produces a lot of wool _because (or) since_ ranchers raise more sheep than other animals.

3. People had been living there for thousands of years _when (or) before_ the first European traders arrived in the 1600s.

4. _After (or) When_ Captain Cook arrived in 1770, the land was claimed for England.

5. Australians live along the coasts _where (or) because (or) since_ the climate is mild.

6. _Until (or) Before_ TV broadcast the 2000 Olympics in Sydney, many people had never seen Australia.

7. There are some zoos in the United States _where_ visitors can see animals from Australia.

8. These zoos have Australian trees _so that_ the animals will feel _as though (or) as if_ they were at home.

Next Step: Write a short description of a place you have read about or seen on TV. Write at least three complex sentences using subordinating conjunctions.

Parts of Speech Review

The English language has eight parts of speech including nouns, verbs, adjectives, adverbs, etc. They help us to understand how we should use words in sentences. The boxes on this page review all the parts of speech and give examples.

Directions ▶ Each box contains a group of words representing one of the eight parts of speech. Write the correct part of speech for each word group on the blank in each box.

round
purple
bright
empty

adjective

later
roughly
very
easily

adverb

hey
oops
great
wow

interjection

our
you
it
mine

pronoun

under
against
upon
around

preposition

shirt
Detroit
elephants
books

noun

though
since
and
but

conjunction

dance
underline
study
write

verb

                                         adjective   *noun*

1   George Washington Carver was a famous African American scientist.

                     adjective

2   He made many important discoveries about plants and farming methods.

        preposition   *noun*   *adverb*

3   He was born on a farm in Missouri and was a very small and sickly child.

  interjection   *preposition*

4   "Oh dear, what will become of this baby?" Mrs. Carver wondered.

                                   conjunction *pronoun*

5   As a little boy, George loved plants and flowers. He knew how to help

                                            conjunction

6   things grow. People called him "the Plant Doctor" because he could make

                 adverb   *pronoun*

7   roses bloom more beautifully than anyone else. He loved to learn about

                            noun   *pronoun*

8   growing things and wanted an education very much. He studied agriculture

                                 preposition

9   at Iowa State University and graduated in 1894.

10   In 1896, another famous African American, Booker T. Washington,

  verb

11   asked Carver to move to Alabama to teach. The Tuskegee Institute was a

                                                   noun

            preposition

12   new school for African Americans. George Washington Carver happily

                                           adverb

                                     verb   *adjective*

13   taught there for more than 40 years. He developed hundreds of new

                   conjunction   *verb*

14   products from peanuts, soybeans, and sweet potatoes. He made paper,

                          adjective

15   plastics, rubber, dyes, and many other products. Before he died at 79,

16   George Washington Carver was invited to meet President Roosevelt. A

            pronoun

17   museum in his honor was set up at the Tuskegee Institute. People wanted a

           conjunction *adverb*   *interjection*

18   statue of him, but he quickly said, "Oh no, I'm not ready to be a monument

                                         verb

19   yet." George Washington Carver was a great scientist. Carver's discoveries

20   have changed our world.

Proofreader's Guide

The following pages present basic rules and examples for punctuation, mechanics, usage, spelling, and grammar. Check here whenever you have an editing and proofreading question.

Marking Punctuation

Period

A **period** is used to end a sentence. It is also used after initials, after abbreviations, and as a decimal point.

To End a Sentence	Use a period to end a sentence that is a statement, a command, or a request. **Computers are getting smaller.** (statement) **Get your pocket computer.** (command) **Please remember extra batteries.** (request)
After an Initial	Use a period after an initial. (An *initial* is the first letter of a name.) **B. B. King** (blues musician)　**Octavia E. Butler** (writer)
As a Decimal Point	Use a period as a decimal point and to separate dollars and cents. **Food prices have risen 48.2 percent.** **Ice-cream cones now cost $1.20.**
After Abbreviations	Place a period after each part of an abbreviation—unless the abbreviation is an acronym. (An *acronym* is a word that is formed from the first letters of words in a phrase.) *Abbreviations*: **Mr.　Mrs.　Jr.　Dr.　U.S.A.** *Acronyms:* **UNICEF　NATO　laser　modem** When an abbreviation is the last word in a sentence, use one period at the end of the sentence. **Supercomputers will be able to predict rain, snow, earthquakes, etc.**

Question Mark

A **question mark** is used at the end of an interrogative sentence. (An *interrogative sentence* asks a question.)

Direct Question	A question mark is used at the end of a direct question (an interrogative sentence). **Will computers help make cars safer?**
Indirect Question	No question mark is used after an indirect question. (In an *indirect question,* you tell about the question you or someone else asked.) **I asked if cars will change a lot.**
Tag Question	A question mark is used when you add a short question to the end of a statement. (This type of statement is called a *tag question.*) **In the next century no one will carry around money, will they?** **People will miss the sound of coins, don't you think?**

Exclamation Point

An **exclamation point** is used to express strong feeling. It may be placed after a word, a phrase, or an exclamatory sentence.

Excellent!   **Wow! That's great!**

Note: Never write more than one exclamation point in school writing assignments or in business letters.

I can't wait to surf the Internet!!! (too many exclamation points)

Comma

Commas keep words and ideas from running together. They make writing easier to read.

Items in a Series

Commas are used between words or phrases in a series. (A *series* contains at least three words or phrases in a row.)

In the future, robots will cook, clean, and iron. (words in a series)

Robots will take out the trash, return phone calls, and open the front door. (phrases in a series)

To Keep Numbers Clear

Commas are used in numbers of four digits or more to keep the numbers clear.

More than 700,000 immigrants enter the United States each year.

When a number refers to a year, street address, or ZIP code, no comma is used. Also, write numbers in the millions and billions this way: 7.5 million, 16 billion.

Brazil, a country of 160 million people, is the largest country in South America.

In Dates and Addresses

Commas are used to set off the different parts in addresses and dates.

Do not use a comma to separate the state from the ZIP code.

My address is 2463 Bell Street,
Kansas City, Missouri 64111.

We will have my birthday party on June 2, 2004, at the roller rink.

Do not use a comma if only the month and year are written (June 2010).

To Set Off Dialogue

Use a comma to set off the words of the speaker from the rest of the sentence.

Writer H. G. Wells once said, "The house of 2000 will have self-cleaning windows."

If you are telling what someone has said but are not using the person's exact words, do not use commas or quotation marks.

Writer H. G. Wells once said that houses in 2000 would have self-cleaning windows.

Comma

To Set Off Interruptions	Commas are used to set off a word or phrase that interrupts the main thought of a sentence. (*Interrupt* means "to break into" or "to stop.") **Computers can, for example, teach people how to play the trumpet or drive a car.** Here is a list of words and phrases you can use to interrupt main thoughts: *for example, however, moreover, to be sure, as a matter of fact, in fact.* Try one of these tests to see if a word or phrase interrupts a main thought: **1.** Take the word or phrase out. The meaning of the sentence should not change. **2.** Move the word or phrase to another place in the sentence. The meaning should not change.
To Set Off Interjections	A comma may be used to separate an interjection from the rest of the sentence. (An *interjection* is a word or phrase showing surprise.) **No kidding, computers may be worn like a wristwatch someday?** **Oh my, I see everything in 3-D!** If an interjection shows very strong feeling, an exclamation point (!) may be used to separate it from the rest of a sentence. Here are some of the words that may be used as interjections: *hello, hey, oh my, no kidding, really, wow.*
In Direct Address	Commas are used to separate a noun of direct address from the rest of the sentence. (A *noun of direct address* names the person being spoken to.) **I know that, Maria. Computers will work with voice commands.**
To Set Off Titles or Initials	Commas are used to set off titles or initials that follow a person's last name. **Gita Punwani, M.D., and Charles K. Robinson, Ph.D., are learning Spanish.** (titles following names) **But Kwon, B. J., and Rodriguez, T. C., are learning French.** (initials following names) If an initial comes at the end of a statement, use only one period.
In Compound Sentences	A comma is used before the connecting word in a compound sentence. (A *compound sentence* is made up of two or more independent clauses connected by words like *and, but, so, nor,* and *yet.*) **Computer technology will help you learn other languages, and it will translate information for you, as well.**

Comma

To Separate Introductory Phrases and Clauses	A comma should be used to separate a longer phrase or a clause that comes *before* the main part of the sentence. **For the first time in recorded history, hunger could be ended everywhere on earth.** (phrase) **If governments would work together, food could be distributed to everyone suffering from hunger.** (clause) You usually do not need a comma when the phrase or the clause comes *after* the main part of the sentence. **Hunger could be ended everywhere on earth for the first time in recorded history.** You usually do not need a comma after a brief opening phrase: **In time soybeans and sea vegetables will be used to feed the world.** (No comma is needed after "in time.")
To Separate Adjectives	Commas are used to separate two or more adjectives that modify a noun in an equal way. (*Equal* means "at the same level" or "of the same type.") **There are plenty of nutritious, edible plants in the world.** ("Nutritious" and "edible" are separated by a comma because they equally modify "plants.") **We may eat many unusual plants in the years to come.** ("Many" and "unusual" do not modify "plants" equally. No comma is needed between these two modifiers.) Use one of these tests to help you decide if adjectives modify equally: **1.** Switch the order of the adjectives. If the sentence is still clear, the adjectives modify equally. **2.** Put the word *and* between the adjectives. If the sentence sounds clear, the adjectives modify equally. *Remember:* Do not use a comma to set off the last adjective from the noun. **Will these unusual plants help solve the terrible, tragic problem of world hunger?** (No comma should be placed between "tragic" and "problem.")
To Set Off Explanatory Phrases	Commas are used to set off an explanatory phrase from the rest of the sentence. (*Explanatory* means "helping to explain.") **Sonja, back from a visit to Florida, told us about new sources of energy.** **Our class, eager to hear her report, listened very carefully.** **Sonja's information, almost all about solar power, was very interesting.**

Comma

To Set Off Appositive Phrases	Commas are used to set off an appositive phrase from the rest of the sentence. (An *appositive phrase* renames the noun or pronoun before it.) **Mrs. Chinn, our science teacher, says that the sun is an important source of energy.** ("Our science teacher" is an appositive phrase.) **Solar power and wind power, two very clean sources of energy, should be used more than they are currently.** ("Two very clean sources of energy" is an appositive phrase.)
To Set Off Nonrestrictive Phrases and Clauses	Commas are used to set off nonrestrictive phrases and clauses from the rest of the sentence. (*Nonrestrictive* means "not necessary.") **Our usable water supply, which comes from surface water or groundwater, makes up only one percent of the total water available on earth.** (The clause "which comes from surface water or groundwater" is nonrestrictive, or not necessary to understand the basic sentence.) No commas are needed before or after a restrictive phrase or clause. (*Restrictive* means "limiting" or "necessary.") **Groundwater that is free from harmful chemicals is hard to find.** (The clause "that is free from harmful chemicals" is restrictive, or necessary to complete the meaning of the sentence.)

Semicolon

	A **semicolon** is sometimes used in the same way that a comma is used. However, a semicolon usually means a stronger pause, closer to a full stop.
To Join Two Independent Clauses	A semicolon can be used to join two independent clauses when there is no connecting word like *and* or *but*. (*Independent clauses* are simple sentences that can stand alone.) **In the future, some cities may rest on the ocean floor; other cities may float like islands.**
With Conjunctive Adverbs	A semicolon is used when two independent clauses are joined by a conjunctive adverb (*also, as a result, besides, for example, however, in addition, instead, meanwhile, moreover, nevertheless, similarly, then, therefore, thus*). The semicolon comes before the adverb, and a comma comes after it. **Living in a floating city sounds interesting; however, living in a city on the ocean floor sounds impossible.**
To Separate Groups That Contain Commas	A semicolon is used to set off groups of words in a series if part of the series already contains commas. **People in the future may live in spacious, comfortable domes; in large, bright space stations; or in underground tunnel cities.**

Colon

A **colon** maybe used to introduce a quotation or a list. Colons are also used in business letters and between the numbers expressing time.

To Introduce a Quotation

A colon may be used to introduce a quotation. (A *quotation* is someone else's exact words that you repeat in your writing.)

President Lincoln made this announcement in his Emancipation Proclamation: "On the 1st day of January, A.D. 1863, all persons held as slaves . . . shall be then, thenceforward, and forever free."

To Introduce a List

A colon is used to introduce a list.

The following materials can be used to build houses: plants, shells, sod, and sand.

When introducing a list, the colon often comes after summary words like *the following* or *these things*.

Computers in the home will do these things: control the lighting, regulate the heating, and provide security.

It is incorrect to use a colon after a verb or a preposition.

Most houses today are made of: brick, wood, stone, or plaster. (The colon is incorrectly used after the preposition "of.")

In a Business Letter

A colon is used after the salutation or greeting in a business letter.

Dear Ms. Kununga: Dear Sir:

Between Numbers in Time

A colon is used between the parts of a number that show time.

7:30 a.m.   12:00 noon   1:00 p.m.   8:45 p.m.

Hyphen

A **hyphen** is used to divide a word at the end of a line. It is also used to form compound words and to write fractions. In addition, a hyphen is used to join the words in compound numbers from twenty-one to ninety-nine, to join letters and words, and so on.

To Divide a Word

A hyphen is used to divide a word when you run out of room at the end of a line. A word may be divided only between syllables (*ex-plor-er*). Here are some additional guidelines. Always refer to a dictionary if you're not sure how to divide a word.

- Never divide a one-syllable word: *would, large,* etc.
- Try not to divide a word of five or fewer letters: *older, habit,* etc.
- Never divide a one-letter syllable from the rest of the word: *apart-ment* not *a-partment.*
- Never divide abbreviations or contractions: *Mrs., Dr., haven't,* etc.

Hyphen

In a Compound Word	A hyphen is used to make some compound words. on-line file search high-speed modem
Between Numbers in a Fraction	A hyphen is used between the numbers in a fraction that is written as a word. one-half (1/2) five-tenths (5/10)
To Join Letters and Words	A hyphen is often used to join a letter to a word. T-shirt X-ray e-mail U-turn
With *Self, Ex, All, Great*	A hyphen is used to form new words beginning with the prefixes *all, self, ex, great*, etc. A hyphen is also used with suffixes such as *elect* and *free*. all-around good student all-knowing teacher ex-hero great-grandmother self-respect self-cleaning oven president-elect smoke-free
To Form an Adjective	Use a hyphen to join two or more words that work together to form a single adjective. voice-recognition software on-screen directions

Dash

	A **dash** is used to show a break in a sentence or to emphasize a word or a group of words.
To Show a Sudden Break	A dash can show a sudden break in a sentence. Because of computers, our world—and the way we describe it—has changed greatly.
For Emphasis	A dash may be used to emphasize a word, a series of words, a phrase, or a clause. You can learn about many subjects—customs, careers, sports, weather—on the Internet.
In Interrupted Speech	Use a dash to show that someone's speech is being interrupted by another person. Well, hello—yes, I—that's right—yes, I—sure, I'd love to—I'll be there!

Quotation Marks

Quotation marks are used for each of the following reasons:
- To set off the exact words of a speaker from the rest of the sentence.
- To show the exact words a writer has quoted from a book or magazine.
- To set off certain titles.
- To set off words used in a special way.

To Set Off the Exact Words of a Speaker	Quotation marks are used to set off a speaker's words in dialogue. **Martha asked, "Who can show me how to find more information about Mexico?"**
To Set Off Quoted Materials	Quotation marks are placed before and after the exact words you quote from magazines and books. **One computer expert said, "In one day the Internet grew by 770 new sites or channels of information."**
To Punctuate Titles	Quotation marks are used to punctuate titles of songs, poems, short stories, book chapters, and articles in encyclopedias, newspapers, or magazines. **"Take Me Out to the Ballgame"** (song) **"Casey at the Bat"** (poem) **"A Game to Remember"** (short story) **"Throwing a Curveball"** (chapter in a book) **"Winning Isn't Everything"** (newspaper article) ✳ When you punctuate a title, capitalize the first word, the last word, and every word in between except for articles (*a, an, the*), short prepositions (*of, for, with*, etc.), and coordinating conjunctions (*and, or, but*, etc.).
Placement of Punctuation	Periods and commas are always placed inside quotation marks. **"You are right," said David. David said, "You are right."** Place an exclamation point or a question mark inside the quotation marks when it punctuates the quotation. **Alfredo asked, "Does anyone want to go for a balloon ride?"** (inside) Place an exclamation point or a question mark outside the quotation marks when it punctuates the main sentence. **Did Alfredo really say, "Balloon rides are better than airplane rides"?** (outside)
Special Words	Use quotation marks around words used in a special way. **I like to "chill out" with my friends.**

Apostrophe

An **apostrophe** is used to form contractions, to form plurals, or to show possession. (*Possession* means "owning something.")

To Form Contractions

An apostrophe is used in a contraction to show that one or more letters have been left out.

couldn't (could not)	he's (he is)	she's (she is)
didn't (did not)	I'll (I will)	they're (they are)
doesn't (does not)	I'm (I am)	won't (will not)
don't (do not)	I've (I have)	wouldn't (would not)
haven't (have not)	it's (it is)	you'd (you would)

To Form Plurals

An apostrophe and *s* are used to form the plural of a letter or a numeral.

A's   B's   3's   10's

To Form Singular Possessives

Form the possessive of most singular nouns by adding an apostrophe and *s*.

Lia's report is on global warming.
It is one of the world's most serious problems.
Mr. Garcia's opinion is different.

When a singular noun ends with an *s* or a *z* sound, the possessive may be formed by adding just an apostrophe.

Carlos' weather chart is very detailed.

But when the singular noun is a one-syllable word, form the possessive by adding both an apostrophe and *s*.

Chris's lab report is incomplete.

To Form Plural Possessives

In most cases, form the possessive of plural nouns ending in *s* by adding just an apostrophe.

The lawmakers' debate dealt with immigration.
The immigrants' first view of the United States was the Statue of Liberty.

For plural nouns not ending in *s*, an apostrophe and *s* must be added.

The children's team practices today.
The men's league starts this weekend.

Remember: The word before the apostrophe is the owner.

Justin's CD (The CD belongs to Justin.)
the girls' uniforms (The uniforms belong to the girls.)

Apostrophe

In Compound Nouns	The possessive of a compound noun is formed by placing the possessive ending after the last word. **his best man's tuxedo** **his sister-in-law's baby**
With Indefinite Pronouns	Form the possessive of an indefinite pronoun (*each, everyone, no one, anyone,* etc.) by adding an apostrophe and *s*. **everyone's idea** **nobody's fault**
To Show Shared Possession	Add an apostrophe and *s* to the last noun when possession is shared. **Sasha and Olga's new science project deals with electricity.**

Italics & Underlining

	Italics is a style of type that is slightly slanted. In this sentence the word *girl* is printed in italics. In handwritten or typed material, each word or letter that should be in italics is underlined. **In *Zlata's Diary* a young girl describes her daily life in Bosnia.** (printed) **In Zlata's Diary a young girl describes her daily life in Bosnia.** (handwritten or typed)
In Titles	Underline (or use italics for) the titles of books, plays, very long poems, magazines, movies, record albums, cassettes, CD's, the names of ships and aircraft, and newspapers. **The Giver** (book) **National Geographic** (magazine) **Babe** (movie) **Andrea Doria** (ship) **Discovery** (spacecraft) **Los Angeles Times** (newspaper)
Foreign Words	Underline (or use italics for) non-English words that are not commonly used in everyday English. Also underline scientific names. **Semper fidelis means "always faithful." It is the motto of the U.S. Marine Corps.**

Parentheses

	Parentheses are used around words that add extra information to a sentence. **You'll pay more for a portable computer (usually called a notebook) than you will for a desktop model.**

Editing for Mechanics

Capitalization

Capitalize all proper nouns and all proper adjectives. A proper noun names a specific person, place, thing, or idea. A proper adjective is an adjective formed from a proper noun.

Common Nouns: **person, country, continent**
Proper Nouns: **Ben Franklin, India, Africa**
Proper Adjectives: **Franklin** stove, **Indian** food, **African** history

Names of People

Capitalize the names of people and also the initials or abbreviations that stand for those names.

Michael Jordan	**Le Duc Anh**
Sigrid Undset	**Benito Juárez**

If a woman uses both her maiden name and married name, the maiden name is listed first, and both are capitalized.

Coretta Scott King	**Kimberly Yashiki Smith**

Women who use two last names often hyphenate them.

Kathleen Aguilera-Pérez	**Margaret Bourke-White**

Historical Names

Capitalize the names of historical documents, events, and periods of time.

World War II   Bronze Age   the Declaration of Independence

Abbreviations

Capitalize titles and abbreviations of organizations.

M.D. (Doctor of Medicine)   **U.S.A.** (United States of America)

Organizations

Capitalize the name of a team, an organization, or an association.

Houston Rockets   International Olympic Committee

Titles Used with Names

Capitalize titles used with names of persons and the abbreviations standing for those titles.

President Bush	**Mayor Martin J. Chavez**
Dr. Amy Lin	**Governor Richards**

Titles

Capitalize the first word of a title, the last word, and every word in between except articles (*a an, the*), short prepositions (*of, at, to,* etc.), and coordinating conjunctions (*and, but, or,* etc.). Follow this rule for titles of books, newspapers, magazines, poems, plays, songs, articles, movies, works of art, stories, and essays.

The Hero and the Crown (book)	**"Kid in the Park"** (poem)
the ***Kansas City Star*** (newspaper)	***Star Wars*** (movie)
Sports Illustrated (magazine)	**"This Land Is Your Land"** (song)
You're a Good Man, Charlie Brown (play)	

Capitalization

First Words

Capitalize the first word of every sentence and the first word in a direct quotation. Do not capitalize the first word in an indirect quotation.

> **Writer** James Berry was born in Jamaica. (sentence)
>
> He explained, **"It's** the function of writers and poets to bring in the left-out side of the human family." (direct quotation)
>
> **Berry said he** writes his stories in Jamaican dialect because it is important to tell these stories in the words of ordinary Jamaicans. (indirect quotation)

Geographic Names

Planets and heavenly bodies	**Earth, Mars, Sirius**
Continents	**Africa, Antarctica, Asia, Australia, Europe, South America**
Countries	**South Korea, Cuba, Rwanda, Poland, Colombia**
States	**Florida, New Jersey, Texas, Illinois, California**
Provinces	**Alberta, British Columbia, Ontario**
Counties	**Cook County, Dade County, Los Angeles County**
Cities	**San Salvador, Nairobi, Tokyo**
Bodies of water	**Lake Michigan, Bay of Bengal, Persian Gulf**
Landforms	**Cape of Good Hope, Mt. Fuji, Mojave Desert, Great Barrier Reef**
Public areas	**Vietnam Memorial, Golden Gate Bridge**
Roads and highways	**Eisenhower Expressway, Lake Shore Drive, Route 66**
Buildings	**Taj Mahal, Mosque of Omar, the White House**

Particular Sections of the Country

Capitalize words that indicate particular sections of the country.

> A large part of the U.S. population lives on the **East Coast.** ("East Coast" is a section of the country.)

Do not capitalize words that simply indicate direction.

> If you keep driving **west**, you will end up in the Pacific Ocean. (direction)

Capitalize proper adjectives formed from the names of specific sections of a country.

> **Eastern** schools
>
> **Southern** cooking

Do not capitalize adjectives formed from words that simply indicate direction.

> the **northern** part of Michigan   driving into **western** Brazil

Capitalization

Names of Languages, Religions, Nationalities, Races

Capitalize the names of languages, religions, nationalities, and races, as well as the proper adjectives formed from them.

Spanish, Urdu, Serbian (languages)

Islam, Christianity, Buddhism (religions)

Chinese, Italian, Polish (nationalities)

Asian, African, European (races)

Japanese twig tea

Ecuadoran coffee

Words Used as Names

Capitalize words such as *mother, father, aunt,* and *uncle* when these words are used as names.

This summer **Aunt Natasha** is taking night classes in English at the high school. ("Aunt Natasha" is the name of a person.)

Father and **Mother** decided to take the class, too. ("Father" and "Mother" are used as names.)

I asked, "**Father**, have you done your homework?" ("Father" is used as a name.)

Words such as *dad, uncle, mother, grandma,* etc., are not usually capitalized if they come after a possessive pronoun (*my, his, our*).

My **father** nodded. He and my **mother** are the best students in the class. ("My father" and "my mother" are not used as names.)

Days of the Week

Capitalize the names of days of the week, months of the year, and special holidays.

Monday   **June**   **New Year's Day**   **Easter**

Do not capitalize the names of seasons.

winter   **spring**   **summer**   **fall** (or autumn)

Official Names

Capitalize the names of businesses and the official names of their products. (These are called trade names.) Do not, however, capitalize a general, descriptive word like *tissues* when it follows the product name.

Duracell batteries   **Timex** watches   **Kleenex** tissues

Capitalize	Do Not Capitalize
American	anti-American
June, October	summer, fall
Senn High School	a high school in Chicago
Governor Christine Todd Whitman	Christine Todd Whitman, our governor
President George Bush	George Bush, our president
Honda Civic LS	a Honda car
We live on planet **Earth.**	The earth we live on is good.
I'm taking **Introduction to Algebra.**	It is a pre-algebra class.

Tenses of Verbs

The time of a verb is called its **tense**. Tense is shown by endings (*talked*), by helping verbs (*did talk*), or by both (*have talked*).

Present Tense

The present tense of a verb states an action that *is happening now* or that *happens regularly*.

> Today, we **honor** Tubman's work.
> She **serves** as an inspiration for all of us.

Past Tense

The past tense of a verb states an action that *happened at a specific time in the past*.

> Ms. Tubman **made** 19 rescue trips. She even **rescued** her parents.

Future Tense

The future tense of a verb states an action that *will take place*.

> I **will remember** her story forever.

Perfect Tense

Present Perfect Tense

The present perfect tense of a verb states an action that *began in the past and is still going on*. Add *has* or *have* before the past participle form of the main verb.

> Stories about slavery **have** always **interested** me.

Past Perfect Tense

The past perfect tense of a verb states an action that *began and was completed in the past*. Add *had* before the past participle form of the main verb.

> She **had served** in the Civil War.

Future Perfect Tense

The future perfect tense of a verb states an action that *will begin in the future and end at a specific time in the future*. Add *will have* before the past participle form of the main verb.

> I **will have studied** for three hours.

Forms of Verbs

Regular Verbs

Most verbs in the English language are regular. To state a past action you add *ed* to regular verbs or use *has, have,* or *had* with the verb.

> **REGULAR VERBS**   I **listen**. Earlier I **listened**. I **have listened**.

Irregular Verbs

Some verbs in the English language are irregular. Usually you do not add *ed* to an irregular verb when you state a past action or use *has, have,* or *had* with the verb. Instead of adding *ed*, the word changes. (See chart on page 184.)

> **IRREGULAR VERBS**   I **speak**. Earlier I **spoke**. I have **spoken**.
>
> She **runs**. Earlier she **ran**. She has **run**.

Common Irregular Verbs

Present Tense	Past Tense	Past Participle	Present Tense	Past Tense	Past Participle
be (am, is, are)	was, were	been	lose	lost	lost
begin	began	begun	make	made	made
bite	bit	bitten	meet	met	met
blow	blew	blown	pay	paid	paid
break	broke	broken	put	put	put
bring	brought	brought	read	read	read
build	built	built	ride	rode	ridden
burst	burst	burst	ring	rang	rung
buy	bought	bought	rise	rose	risen
catch	caught	caught	run	ran	run
choose	chose	chosen	say	said	said
come	came	come	see	saw	seen
cost	cost	cost	sell	sold	sold
cut	cut	cut	send	sent	sent
dive	dove, dived	dived	set	set	set
do	did	done	shake	shook	shaken
draw	drew	drawn	shine (light)	shone	shone
drink	drank	drunk	shrink	shrank	shrunk
drive	drove	driven	sing	sang	sung
eat	ate	eaten	sink	sank	sunk
fall	fell	fallen	sit	sat	sat
feel	felt	felt	speak	spoke	spoken
fight	fought	fought	spend	spent	spent
find	found	found	spin	spun	spun
fly	flew	flown	spread	spread	spread
freeze	froze	frozen	spring	sprang	sprung
get	got	got, gotten	stand	stood	stood
give	gave	given	steal	stole	stolen
go	went	gone	swear	swore	sworn
grow	grew	grown	swim	swam	swum
hang (suspend)	hung	hung	swing	swung	swung
hide	hid	hidden	take	took	taken
hit	hit	hit	teach	taught	taught
hold	held	held	tear	tore	torn
hurt	hurt	hurt	tell	told	told
keep	kept	kept	think	thought	thought
know	knew	known	throw	threw	thrown
lay (place)	laid	laid	wake	woke	woken
lead	led	led		waked	waked
leave	left	left	wear	wore	worn
lend	lent	lent	weave	wove	woven
let	let	let	win	won	won
lie (recline)	lay	lain	write	wrote	written

Common Two-Word Verbs

This chart lists verbs in which two words work together to express a specific action.

break down . . . . take apart or fall apart
call off . . . . cancel
call up . . . . make a phone call
clear out . . . . leave a place quickly
cross out . . . . draw a line through
do over . . . . repeat
figure out . . . . find a solution
fill in/out . . . . complete a form or an application
fill up . . . . fill a container or tank
find out . . . . discover
get in . . . . enter a vehicle
get out of . . . . leave a car, a house, or a situation
get over . . . . recover from a sickness or a problem
give back . . . . return something
give in/up . . . . surrender or quit
hand in . . . . give homework to a teacher
hand out . . . . give someone something
hang up . . . . put down a phone receiver
leave out . . . . omit or don't use
let in/out . . . . allow someone or something to enter or go out
look up . . . . find information
mix up . . . . confuse
pay back . . . . return money or a favor
pick out . . . . choose
point out . . . . call attention to
put away . . . . return something to its proper place
put down . . . . place something on a table, the floor, etc.
put off . . . . delay doing something
shut off . . . . turn off a machine or light
take part . . . . participate
talk over . . . . discuss
think over . . . . consider carefully
try on . . . . put on clothing to see if it fits
turn down . . . . lower the volume
turn up . . . . raise the volume
write down . . . . write on a piece of paper

✳ Usually, do not divide a two-word verb in a sentence. For example, write "I *handed out* the papers," not "I *handed* the papers *out*."

ADJECTIVES

An **adjective** is a word that modifies (describes) nouns or pronouns. Adjectives tell *what kind, how many,* or *which one.*

> **rainy   green   smooth   twelve   wonderful**

- **Articles** are special adjectives. There are three articles: *a, an,* and *the. (An* usually comes before singular words that begin with a vowel and *a* before words that begin with a consonant or long "u.")

- **Proper adjectives** are formed from proper nouns and are always capitalized. Common adjectives are any adjectives that are not proper (and not capitalized).

  The **Italian** scientist Galileo was the **first** person to see sunspots.

ADVERBS

An **adverb** is a word that modifies (describes) verbs, adjectives, or other adverbs. Adverbs tell *how, when, where, how often,* and *how much.*

> **slowly   yesterday   here   daily   more**

INTERJECTIONS

An **interjection** is a word or phrase that expresses strong emotion. Commas or exclamation marks are used to separate interjections from the rest of the sentence.

> **Stop! Hey**, how are you?   **For goodness sake**, let's get going!

PREPOSITIONS

A **preposition** is a word that shows position or direction and introduces a prepositional phrase.

> **about   up   inside   upon   between   to**

- A **prepositional phrase** includes a preposition, the object of the preposition (the noun or pronoun that comes after the preposition), and any words that modify the object.

  The coolest parts **of your body** are your fingers and toes. (The word "of" is a preposition, "body" is the object of the preposition, and "your" is a modifier.)

CONJUNCTIONS

A **conjunction** is a word that connects individual words or groups of words. There are three kinds of conjunctions.

Coordinating: **and, but, or, nor, for, so, yet**

Correlative: **either/or, neither/nor, not only/but also, both/and, whether/or, as/so**

Subordinating: **after, although, as, as if, as long as, as though, because, before, if, in order that, since, so, so that, though, unless, until, when, where, whereas, while**